GO OUTSIDE

GO OUTSIDE

get up. get out. change the world.

Alton Lee Webb

Fedd Books
P.O. Box 341973
Austin, TX 78734
www.thefeddagency.com

Published in association with The Fedd Agency, Inc., a literary agency.

Unless otherwise noted, all scripture quotations are from the ESV® Bible(The Holy
Bible, English Standard Version®), copyright © 2001 by Crossway, a publishing
ministry of Good News Publishers. Used by permission. All rights reserved.

Scriptures taken from the Holy Bible, New International Version®, NIV®. Copyright
© 1973, 1978, 1984, 2011 by Biblica, Inc.™ Used by permission of Zondervan. All
rights reserved worldwide. www.zondervan.com The "NIV" and "New International
Version" are trademarks registered in the United States Patent and Trademark Office
by Biblica, Inc.™

The opinions and conclusions expressed in this book are those of the author. All
references to websites, blogs, authors, publications, brand names and/or products are
placed there by the author.

This publication is designed to provide accurate and authoritative information with
regard to the subject matter covered. It is sold with the understanding that the publisher
or author is not engaged in rendering finacial, accounting, or other professional advice,
If financial advice or other expert assitance is required, the services of a competent
professional should be sought.

ISBN: 978-1-943217-25-0
eISBN: 978-1-943217-26-7
Cover design by Lauren Hall
Photography by Rachel Lee Webb, Kendra Kiser, and Laura Coppelman Photography
Go Outside back cover logo by Nathan Morgan
Printed in the United States of America

First Edition 15 14 13 10 09 / 10 9 8 7 6 5 4 3 2

For my encouraging wife, Rachel,
who loves people authentically, and
my three children who are true delights from God.

CONTENTS

My Outsider Story 11

Elements of Going Outside 17

Element One: Essentials

Discover Your Bird Cage 21

Bearing Disgrace 27

Be Epic. Not Perfect. 33

Portrait of an Outsider 37

Maher-Shalal-Hash-Baz 45

Element Two: Vision

Questionable Foot-washing 53

Ponyboy and the "In Crowd" 57

Welcome to Whoville 63

The Dream of the Nineties is Alive in Shelbyville 69

The Cash Cow is Bull 75

Element Three: Learning

Learning to Unlearn 81

Wallpaper Border and Lavender Paint 87

Code of Silence   93

Be Ready for Curveballs   99

Element Four: Logistics

Don't Quit Your Day Job (Unless You Need To)   105

Find a Paint Store   111

At a Crossroads   115

Beware of Insiders   121

Element Five: Beyond

Bad Idea   129

Don't Let the Door Hit You On Your Way Out (Literally)   137

Keep Out.   143

Squad Goals   147

Not the Conclusion

The Great Commission   161

Jesus the Ultimate Outsider   169

Join the Outsider Movement   175

Acknowledgments   179
About the Author   181
Endnotes   183
Notes   185

"They grew up on the outside of society.
They weren't looking for a fight.
They were looking to belong."

– S.E. Hinton, *The Outsiders*

MY OUTSIDER STORY

I lay in bed wide awake in the darkness of an early July morning in 2009. My wife was still in a deep sleep, so I found a place of solitude and a little light to read my Bible amongst the smelly laundry in my closet. In that odd and tight place, I read a passage that would change my entire family's life.

As I read the words on the thin, almost transparent pages, I had a feeling that something huge was happening—and then it hit me. I shot up. After pushing clothes aside, tripping over shoes and getting hit in the face with a belt, I ran over to my sleeping wife, and shook Rachel hard.

"This is IT!"

With tired eyes, she said, "What!!??"

I continued, "It's right here, this passage. It's my heart." Rachel said, "I love you, but what does that mean?" In the past, she carried loads of conversations like this so patiently. (You know, the one-sided talks filled with passion but no starting points or details?) It all seemed to go nowhere. She gave me a sheepish smile and turned over. I thought, *I have no idea "what" this is, but it has had a terrific effect on me.*

Usually when I shoot out of bed it's because my kids are poking my head, tugging my hair, and yelling in my ear, "Get up, daddy!" My kids love to play outside. If they hear the garage door open or sniff fresh air – no matter the time of day—they get up and rush to the nearest exit. "Daddy! Daddy, let's *go*!" Inquisitive little faces. Opportunities for grand adventures devour their minds. "I can make a battleship in the driveway! It's time to take all my babies on a red wagon ride to the beach! Wonder if my boomerang can go over the house and come back? The cool stuff is out there, and I'm in here. Let me *out*!"

So the next morning when I opened the front door, the kiddos piled outside, and much to our neighbors early-morning chagrin, they were set free. As I watched their joy, innocent curiosity, and imagination unfolding, I wanted the same thing. I could vaguely remember the feeling of such release. But, life is tough and it's easy to be a cynic. I turned and looked at the coffee pot and wondered, "How could those days ever return?"

Then the scripture hit me all over again.

It was as if a refrigerator, still in its cardboard delivery box, was lifted off my world-weary thinking. I don't *have* to spend life inside. I don't *have* to settle for consistency and familiarity. Life was much more than something just for me. The exploration doesn't stop in my three-bedroom ranch home. That's when it all started. Outside is where I belonged.

Have you ever thought:

I wonder if I could do that?

I would love to see that made better

What we need is_____.

I feel like God might want me to do something about this issue?

It seems as quickly as these thoughts come to us, we are just as swift to shoot them down.

The timing isn't right for me.

I'd be the laughing stock of the world if it crashed.

I got burned last time, plus, I just don't have the money.

What happens if I actually succeed?

Our passion slips and down goes our courage. Our comfort zone and busyness drown the dream. We stop the exploration before it even starts. We think, *maybe it was just too much coffee.*

So we settle. We stay inside.

But maybe you're tired of letting this happen. Maybe this time it will be different. Maybe you've decided the normal roadblocks thwarting the future, have led you to this moment. Maybe "going Outside" is more than just a wild idea. Maybe this is not a fleeting ambition, but a prompting. A calling to get up, to get out, and to change the world.

I'm an everyday guy. I live in a small town in Central Kentucky. I have three kids and a rescue dog who likes to pee on stuff. My wife drives a minivan. I drink lots of coffee. Totally average biopic in the making here.

But somehow I've been self-employed for twenty years, which has allowed me to consult on behalf of entrepreneurs and corporate clients, serve on boards, and lead economic development organizations. That makes me a pro. NOT. Heck, that same idea of wanting to go Outside into the great unknown— of thinking maybe I could and should do this—is still something that gives me indigestion. Perhaps, that's why I like it. (Not the stomach stuff, but the perceived opportunity.) I'm a starter. I love the challenge of overcoming difficulty. Hearing "no" motivates me—I just won't rest until things are made better. The question always looms, "If I don't do this, who will?" For me, going Outside is not an option. It's an urgent mandate.

That's why these words hit me so hard in my closet at the crack of dawn on that July morning:

"For the bodies of those animals whose blood is brought into the holy places by the high priest as a sacrifice for sin are burned outside the camp. So Jesus also suffered outside the gate in order to sanctify the people through his own blood. Therefore **let us go to him outside the camp** *and bear the reproach he endured. For here we have no lasting city, but we seek the city that is to come. Through him then let us continually offer up a sacrifice of praise to God, that is, the fruit of lips that acknowledge his name."* (Hebrews 13:11-15, emphasis mine).

Look. I get it. These aren't verses that usually get a lot of attention. They won't be found on the black eye grease applied to a football player's face this Saturday. They won't be found on a DIY chalkboard painting in someone's "pinnable" kitchen. And as for me, I felt like a real weirdo for being drawn to a section of the Bible that started off with a high priest, animal blood, sin offerings, and burnings. Honestly, that's disgusting and not exactly dinner table conversation. Why couldn't I have rested in the green pastures of Psalm 23, or the strength of Philippians 4:13? I memorized John 3:16 before I was old enough to read, why not land there? Why did that passage in Hebrew 13 grab me by the collar?

As I allowed my mind to mull and brew over the imagery, the horror, the injustice, the intensity, the connection to the former way of dealing with our extreme inadequacy, the joy of the potential journey, Outside became more and more alive.

I was captivated.

I started to see the classics, Psalm 23, Philippians 4:13, and John 3:16, show up in Hebrews 13. Everything I prayed about was summed up right there—my delights, the passion, the struggle, and my calling. Jesus went Outside for me. He bore my disgrace. But not for me to stay put. I could see Him standing at the door, grinning and waving me towards the Outside and the adventure He had for me. It struck me inalterably, but I felt neither burdened nor intimidated.

In these brief moments, I became an Outsider. Not politically or like a character in a bad Netflix series. There were no catchy slogans or bucket list adventures in my mind. It was all simple, really. Every time I read the passage, I took a step toward Him. I heard His voice clearly (step) and the only way to respond was to come closer (step, step, step). I just wanted to be with Him.

Life was bliss until I discovered that the nearer I moved toward Him, the further I moved outside the city limits of my neat and happy suburban life.

As we attended church the next Sunday, the contented spot I enjoyed for decades became my distress. I looked up at the well-appointed chandeliers. I was lost in their intricacies and in my thoughts. *I'm not supposed to be here anymore, but where will I go, what will I do? I love this place and these people. I was raised here, married here, and we had our first child dedicated here.* God was working here, but he was relentlessly pulling me somewhere else and it was suffocating.

Trying to breathe, I grabbed the half pencil beside the hymnal, barely sharpened with the eraser chewed off, and stared at the church bulletin. It was like no one else was in the room. My mind was flooded with faces and stories of people who would probably never step foot in a church. I didn't know what to do, so I started writing. Nothing was fully-formed or made sense. It was just a page full of questions. That traditional church pew was getting more and more uncomfortable.

Then, as if God wasn't speaking already, the words of our pastor boomed me back to reality, "Some of you might need to lead new works and new ministries to reach new people." I felt my heart burst open, shoving my anxiety and uncertainty aside. I started writing names. Lots and lots of them.

I looked around and saw my family, my close friends—wonderful people who loved me, who had invested in me. Until that morning, it seemed like everything I needed was inside those walls, but everything in me was telling me something much different. GET OUT. I twisted away and, in an alarmingly too-loud-for-church voice, said "No way."

Going Outside often starts small—a desire for change, a crazy concept or a pesky idea that doesn't go away. It's the realization that a dream will stay just that if we fail to take action in our daily lives. It's getting off the bench and in the game. Outside often takes us to the uncomfortable—away from familiarity—towards people we normally wouldn't be associated with. It unfolds beyond temporal or practical thinking. In fact, going Outside is best fueled by the haphazard idea to serve others at all costs.

Simply put, to go Outside is to leave yourself behind.

As I sat in that pew, I felt smothered by my perfectly-crafted Christian life. I wrote one last question and passed it to Rachel, "Do we have a greater chance of reaching those Outside by leaving or by staying here?" Her face said it all.

As the worship service came to a close, the friendly faces that welcomed us each Sunday smiled and told us they would see us next week. I had a pit in my stomach because I knew once we stepped Outside, we wouldn't be back.

ELEMENTS OF GOING OUTSIDE

In my journey Outside, I've learned alongside others who have been mining the elements and discovering the key ingredients to what an Outsider needs.

Outside is an expedition. The very thought invokes the idea of braving the traditional five elements; space, earth, air, water, and fire. The Outside analogies seem endless. But, to keep us on track, I'm introducing the following five Outsider elements: essentials, vision, logistics, learning, and beyond.

Essentials are just that. You can't do without them. **Vision** will keep you from losing direction and herding cats. **Logistics** are the questions you'll have early on. **Learning** is a key ingredient to sustainability. **Beyond** is the long-haul view for the journey to become independent of you.

Some of these elements will be applicable in moments; others might be for use much later. You may need more of one element than another for your specific calling. It's also conceivable that some elements will come easier to you than others. They are movable and build upon each other organically as you go.

"I often wonder, why men are satisfied to live all their lives between brick walls and thinking of nothing but money and the so-called recreations of so-called society when there is so much enjoyment in the country."
–James Roosevelt

To help in your journey, take time to experience the stories of fellow Outsiders collected in this book. They will teach you more about the elements and how God has applied them to their lives. I've also included a ton of questions at the end of each chapter that will keep you thinking about your own Outsider journey and a notes section in the back of the book. As God leads you into the open world Outside, it's my hope that these elements come naturally and help you go further than you would have ever thought possible.

"Christians are like manure: Spread them out and they help everything grow better, but keep them in one big pile and they stink horribly."
—Francis Chan

Element One:

Essentials

"For the bodies of those animals whose blood is brought into the holy places by the high priest as a sacrifice for sin are burned **outside** the camp..."

DISCOVER YOUR
BIRD CAGE

Curt Vernon felt like he needed to go pray.

For a living.

Weird.

Especially since Curt slept literally "in a van down by the river." He and a buddy traveled 30,000 miles in eighteen months—driving from Kentucky to California and everywhere in between. Curt said, "For real, all we did was just pray." They'd stop at campuses, restaurants, and churches along the way. Just to pray.

> "Incline your ear, O Lord, and answer me,
> for I am poor and needy.
> Preserve my life, for I am godly;
> save your servant, who trusts in you—you are my God.
> Be gracious to me, O Lord,
> for to you do I cry all the day.
> Gladden the soul of your servant,
> for to you, O Lord, do I lift up my soul."
> Psalm 86:1-4

Curt wasn't raising money. When he needed something, he

would pray. Curt wasn't assembling large groups of people. Curt's heart was for renewal and revival. Many people were impacted by his heart. He taught me that praying was important because it reminded me how much God loved me, and how much I needed Him. It taught me that without a deeper and more abiding relationship with Jesus, I'd "go" nowhere fast.

> *When we work, we work; but when we pray, God works.*
> *– Max Lucado*

But I'm no Curt Vernon. I often find myself praying fervently over small things like a lost phone. (Funny, how many times I actually found it after those prayers!) Maybe for the rest of us we pray mostly over big things, like a financial hardship, a failing relationship, a scary health diagnosis, or a rocky plane ride.

As I struggled with prayer, Rachel started something that has since become a family tradition. Lots of times when we prayed, she would jot the praises or petitions down on scraps of paper and toss them in an old bird cage. This sorry excuse for a decoration suddenly became significant. I didn't think it could hurt, so I joined in. Then it started to get really interesting when we opened a few of the notes months later. The feelings of worry and uncertainty came back to me as I unfolded each one, but I was quickly struck by the outcomes too. Not all of these requests were answered exactly as I had hoped. Some of them don't have answers yet. But our faith in prayer has grown. Confidence that our God is listening continues to give us hope for the future and courage for our "going."

As a parent, one of my deepest fears is something bad happening to one of my children.

Rachel's friend, Jamie, faced my worst nightmare when her seemingly-healthy five-year-old son, Paxton, was diagnosed with the most aggressive form of pediatric cancer, Burkitt Lymphoma, in 2014.

At first, Paxton's pediatrician insisted that nothing was wrong with the lymph node on his neck. He wanted to take a wait-and-see approach. Jamie said, "Our pediatrician thought I was absolutely nuts because his blood work was normal. But I knew the lymph node on his neck was not normal. God told me something was wrong." Jamie said she didn't care if she got arrested; someone was going to see her son, take her seriously, and get the lymph node off of his neck.

If Jamie had not persisted, her son would have died within a few months. Burkitt's cells can multiply every six hours. Time to wait-and-see was something her son did not have.

The next six months of Jamie's life would be a blur of tests and tears and lots and lots of time sleeping in the twin size bed in the hospital room with her son, praying and watching as he lost every hair on his head and battled through painful treatments and procedures.

"It was one of the most horrible experiences, yet God had never felt so real. I would listen to the song, 'Great I Am,' on my phone and pray over him when he went through the scanner. I would feel the physical presence of God and his angels. Everyone wants to know God is near, and we did. We had 30,000 to 40,000 people all over the world praying for us and following our story through our "Paxton Strong" Facebook page. Churches sent blankets. People delivered food that had been prayed over. It was the best and worst experience of my life, all at once."

Prayer transformed Paxton from being diagnosed with stage 4 cancer (the worst in the world) to having him healed on Good Friday (six weeks later). His initial treatment lasted exactly the forty days of lent, something Jamie insists is not a coincidence. "Jesus rose from the grave, and God raised my son from the grave."

Pray without ceasing
- I Thessalonians 5:17

But Jamie said the prayers didn't stop there. Dealing with the post-traumatic stress of Paxton's illness brings waves of depression and isolation, as many don't understand the kind of sadness that her family has walked through. "So many people think my spiritual life is perfect and I have to be perfect in my faith because we have been given this awesome blessing of healing, but it's not. There have been times that I *have* been strong and others when I felt like I would die from a broken heart." But Jamie never stopped praying and believing in the power of God. "I see the full picture of God's plan—devastation and triumph."

"I have a friend whose little girl was recently sent home with no treatment plan to heal her cancer. I see our children playing together and I don't understand why God chose to give the two dramatically different outcomes. But I have to be okay with not always understanding God's plan."

A year and three months after her son's initial diagnosis, Jamie welcomed a third baby into their home—a little girl named Maura, named after Paxton's primary oncologist. "When I look at her, I think, what a blessing. He has already healed my son, and now He has given me a sign that He will restore me and help me to have hope and joy again."

"Prayer is both conversation and encounter with God . . . We must know the awe of praising his glory, the intimacy of finding his grace, and the struggle of asking his help, all of which can lead us to know the spiritual reality of his presence."
– Tim Keller

Moving forward, Jamie continues to turn to prayer when worry creeps in. "We have to give ourselves grace for being human and having fear. Prayer is what gives us hope after a dark time. God speaks through the uncertainty. He whispers "hang on, there are better days coming."

"*Give ear, O Lord, to my prayer; listen to my plea for grace. In the day of my trouble I call upon you, for you answer me. There is none like you among the gods, O Lord, nor are there any works like yours. All the nations you have made shall come and worship before you, O Lord, and shall glorify your name. For you are great and do wondrous things; you alone are God. Teach me your way, O Lord, that I may walk in your truth; unite my heart to fear your name. I give thanks to you, O Lord my God, with my whole heart, and I will glorify your name forever"* (Psalm 86:5-12).

And we know that for those who love God all things work together for good, for those who are called according to his purpose.
– Romans 8:28

As Outsiders, we must learn that prayer is the most imperative part of the journey. Prayer, interwoven with God's word, humbles us, helps us test our motives, and reminds us of who we are and *Whose* we are. It's fuel for *going*. Prayer is our time to be illuminated by the Holy Spirit's leadership for going Outside, which is super indispensable.

Prayer is not the act of convincing God to help you get your idea started; it's recognition that God is the starter of all things good and perfect.

Every good gift and every perfect gift is from above, coming down from the Father of lights with whom there is no variation or shadow due to change.
James 1:17

TAKE ACTION

- Buy a prayer guide. Here's one I use: *Prayers for Today: A Yearlong Journey of Contemplative Prayer* by Kurt Bjorklund
- Identify a place(s) of solitude. Find your routine. Read scripture and just talk with God. Listen. Record your thoughts.
- Read John 16:13-16. How is the Holy Spirit leading

and guiding you as you contemplate going Outside?
- Pray as you go, as you drive, walk from office to office, or clean the kitchen. God is available.

BEARING
DISGRACE

When I was in seventh grade something strange happened. My best friend's voice started to sound much different—like deeeeeeeeper. I can remember him on safety patrol yelling down the hall at running kids thinking he was a grown adult. He started to look different. He wasn't interested in playing any reindeer games with our friends. He started to walk with a swagger instead of skipping down the sidewalks. He had hair on his legs and under his arms. This was absolutely foreign to me. Did something crawl inside of this dude?

As time went on, other friends started to change as well. But nothing was happening to me. So I started to fake it. I would deepen my voice and wear long pants to cover my hairless legs. The boys were becoming men and the girls were becoming women, but I was still the schoolboy.

It was humiliating.

When I entered my freshman year of high school, I was less than 100 pounds and was barely five feet tall. It was odd, but didn't really matter much until it affected the thing I loved most—sports. In middle school, I tried out for basketball. I had the talent and skill level, but not the height, so I didn't make the cut. I was saddened, but I was hopeful that my time would come. I focused on soccer and other sports I enjoyed, but kept working on my hoops game too.

My freshman year, I mustered the courage to try out for the basketball team again. Even though I was smaller than everyone by 7-10 inches, I had the highest free throw and shooting percentages. I was ecstatic when I saw my name on the team roster. I made it! Well, until the day our freshman team scrimmaged the varsity squad. I got manhandled, literally, and the coaches took notice. I was asked to be a manager instead of a player for "safety purposes" and it was devastating. As I shuffled back to my classroom after receiving the news, shame washed over me. I was embarrassed by my size, my lack of manhood, and my insufficient talent. I wept bitterly out loud—I couldn't hold back. I'm sure I sounded like a first grader pouting at his desk. My dream of being a Kentucky basketball player was over if I couldn't make the freshman high school team!

High school went on and, finally, my junior year I would lose my nickname—little Jonny. (Yes, that was the way my affectionate schoolmates referred to me.) *Maybe now I wouldn't be so mortified. Maybe a girl would consider going to a movie with me instead of referring to me as their miniature buddy.* Good news, I did find a date by my senior prom and headed off to college with adult-sized shoes at a soaring height of 5'8".

After years of suffering, it was all good.

One of my favorite outdoor brands has the motto "life is good." Truth is, I know very little about suffering. First off, my family lives in a quintessential middle-class neighborhood in America. Our minivan is covered in half-eaten applesauce pouches and Goldfish crumbs, but it still runs fine. We have closets (and a basement) full of clothes and shoes. If you hear me complaining, please smack me up side the head.

But sometimes life doesn't seem good.

I had to tell my wife that her father passed away unexpectedly at the age of 55. I baptized a young man, only to speak at his funeral when he overdosed a year later. I sat with a mother and a father at the hospital, hours after they lost their baby. I consoled a friend as he relived the painful details of how his marriage fell apart. But, there have been very few times when I have been personally steamrolled by suffering. Perhaps that is why I am still learning the gift of mercy. To feel the pain of others. To sit with them. To cry with them. *Just be with them.*

Most people don't start their morning devotions in Leviticus. It's not been my go to either. But I recently spent a few hours in a hotel lobby reading Leviticus, chapters 13 and 14. I got to this verse:

Seven times he shall sprinkle the one to be cleansed of the defiling disease, and then pronounce them clean. After that, he is to release **the live bird in the open fields.** Leviticus 14:7 (NIV, emphasis mine)

I learned that this was part of the process during the old covenant where the priest would make the unclean, clean. Some believe the bird symbolizes the disease being taken outside the camp—where the unclean must stay until they are clean. That's probably true. But, why would I feel it necessary to focus on the bird in the open fields?

Birds, birds, hmm . . . my mind wondered to Matthew 26 where Jesus teaches us about freedom from worry or anxiety, "the birds of the air that do not sow or reap or store away in barns." It's no coincidence that Rachel and I keep our most private and pressing fears and prayers in a birdcage.

How many times did we see Jesus release people from the chains that held them captive? How about the time Jesus led the blind man Outside by the hand?

They came to Bethsaida, and some people brought a blind man and begged Jesus to touch him. **He took the blind man by the hand and led him outside the village.** *When he had spit on the man's eyes and put his hands on him, Jesus asked, "Do you see anything?" He looked up and said, "I see people; they look like trees walking around." Once more Jesus put his hands on the man's eyes. Then his eyes were opened, his sight was restored, and he saw everything clearly.* Mark 8:22-25 (NIV, emphasis mine.)

There's that word again—Outside, but coupled with release. Why would Jesus take him Outside to heal him? Wasn't it about freedom?

I rushed back to Hebrews 13:13. *"And so Jesus also suffered outside the city gate to make the people holy through his own blood. Let us, then, go to him outside the camp,* **bearing the disgrace he bore.** (NIV, emphasis mine.)

Two words. "Jesus suffered . . ." Torture. Unspeakable Shame. Crucifixion. The severity of it all. *He bore our disgrace.* The agony Jesus went through has to be considered. It can't be glossed over.

The bird, the open fields, seeing everything clearly, the provision, the value that is shown, the view seen outside rather then inside—my mind raced. The essence of going Outside became even more clear.

To go Outside is to leave it all behind in Jesus. The agony he suffered means that we can all be outside of our own pain. We can leave our junk. Our past and future downfalls. Our current battles. The blood of Jesus sets us free. Like a bird in the open air. He takes us outside of our agony to a place where only He can bring solace. To just be with Him—that's Outside enough. As God calls us to take action in the specific mission given to us outside the camp, go because of the disgrace he carried and the freedom only He provides.

"'Sacrifices and offerings, burnt offerings and sin offerings you did not desire, nor were you pleased with them'—though they were offered. Then he said 'Here I am, I have come to do your will.' He sets aside the first to establish the second. And by that will, we have been made holy through the sacrifice of the body of Jesus Christ once for all" (Hebrews 10:8-10 NIV).

One of the first times I met Rachel, she was speaking to the youth group at my church. She was a junior in college. When I saw her walk into the room, it was like time slowed to a crawl and I'm pretty someone was blowing her hair with a fan. Cue "Dream Weaver." She was way out of my league. Seriously, I'm not saying that to sound like a good husband. Ask anyone.

But, you want to know my main concern?

I pondered, *How tall is this girl?* My high school shame came flooding back. I was so concerned that my friend and I actually I came up with a plan to make sure I was at least ¼ inch taller. Turns out I was actually at least two inches taller! Nowadays, we're all good unless she wears those stupid high heels. I have no desire to pimp, but I promise you, if those 70s platform shoes ever came back into serious fashion for men, I'd be the first in line.

TAKE ACTION

- Jesus always finishes the job. Have you allowed him to work on your faults and pain?
- Jesus never leaves us when we go Outside. Has the fear of going alone held you back?
- As you chase the dream God has given you, are you willing to join Him in the disgrace that might come your way?

BE EPIC.
NOT PERFECT.

When I first started my business, I was all about cold calls. I'd reach out to anybody. If you owned some property in my area, you were going to hear from me. But, if I'm being honest, I was embarrassed about the perception I was giving. Did it make me look weak or desperate? What legitimate sales person needed to do this sort of thing? So, I came up with what I thought was the perfect solution. When the calls didn't start off well, I would just lie about my identity. These innocent property owners would exclaim, "Who is this!?" and I'd nervously reply, "Its Joe or Bill from such and such (fake) company." I'd laugh aloud, thinking there was nothing wrong with what I was doing. The joke would eventually be on me.

One such call would turn out to be unforgettable. I didn't think it was going well, so I lied about my identity and hung up. Have you ever heard of Star 69? Busted! The person called me back and said, "I don't know why you hung up. I really was interested, Joe." Of course, I had to come clean. Guess what? I didn't get the job. *Surprise, surprise.*

What was I setting in motion? The long term effects of my technique would keep me up at night. I knew these types of practices could put me out of business quickly—especially in a small town. I had to apologize. I needed to change my ways.

So, from that moment on, I owned the call. I owned the fact that I was just starting.

As my career moved on, I began to enjoy the challenge of prospecting. Taking the initiative to grow my business was nothing to be ashamed of. In the beginning, I was trying to gain quick insights and leads without owning up to the hard parts. I was also wasting my future away. I wasn't building a good reputation or character, which would be essential to opening any future opportunities.

Your character is defined by you and only you. No one can take it away, except for you. Be careful, Outsiders. Your desire for instant success will work against building solid character. Building character is "one choice, one day, one person at a time" stuff. Be judicious. As you head Outside, you'll find it easy to squander your character, whether in public or private.

"When wealth is lost, nothing is lost;
when health is lost, something is lost;
when character is lost, all is lost."
– Billy Graham

Ashley Madison is an online dating service with the slogan "Life is short. Have an affair." As of 2015, the site had millions and millions of hits per month. But something happened. The site was hacked. Not just for credit card information, but also the names and details of the customers using the site. Oh snap. Can you imagine being a married man and the threat of all your discrete adventures being exposed? The life you lived in private would become become public. The character you portrayed would be slayed.

Jesus taught us a lot about integrity—about our lives behind closed doors looking like the lives behind the open ones. He taught us that with good character as a foundation, we can always remain sincere and authentic, and who we are and who we appear to be are one in the same. Using the example of prayer, he taught us to not be like the hypocrites who love to stand on street corners, "so that they may be seen by others." Instead Jesus encouraged us to spend time with our door shut, where we pray in secret. As we spend time in seclusion with God, good character naturally emerges and the internal quest to know Him affects the most public parts of our life. It makes it harder to live with our contradictions.

"If I'm always late to meetings or late picking my kids up from school, what does that say about how I value other people's time?

"If I'm willing to turn my head and plow through a cloudy conscience, how can I expect others to be honest with me?"

"Am I as kind to Rachel in the minivan with kids screaming, as I am in the church foyer greeting new guests?"

As Outsiders, we aren't perfect. I mean come on—there is no *epic* in perfection—oh, wait . . . there is. But still, we must take the challenge of guarding, growing, and promoting solid character both in private and in public life seriously. Just as we privately place our belief and trust in Jesus for salvation, He then teaches us to publicly acknowledge Him before others. The result is even more compelling—he'll do the same for us, but even better. With our private and public trust in Him, he assures us that He will acknowledge us openly before our Father in Heaven.

TAKE ACTION

- As Outsiders, our private life and prayers do a lot to build our public character. At the risk of losing a deal or offending someone, we become more authentic followers of Jesus when we daily invest in our own integrity. Make a list of ways you can start today.
- Read Matthew 6:5-6 and Matthew 10:32-33. List the differences you notice as it relates to building character.
- Are you in an environment or in situations where you've let your guard down? Which website or social

media participation is eating away at solid character, click by click? How can you start to protect and build a consistent private and public life that matches? Ask a friend to help you stay on task, provide insight, potential correction and much needed encouragement.

PORTRAIT OF
AN OUTSIDER

In the little town of Shelbyville, Kentucky, Clay Street is the street *behind* Main Street. In a small town, that's not good. If you're not on a "main" street, you don't get the foot or car traffic that drives economic value. You're not on the chief thorough-fare of downtown revitalization. You are tucked away from the courthouse, the post office, cafés, and most retailers. Clay Street has some traffic, but it doesn't stop. It's a cut-through from one end of the city to the other.

However, Willie Fleming loves everything about Clay Street, a hilly swath of town with shotgun houses, back-building alleys and a few churches. That's why when Rachel called Willie to brainstorm where to take his portrait, there was really no other option. Willie is synonymous with Clay Street.

One day, when Rachel was rushing around to meet with several people in this book to take their portrait, she somehow got times mixed up and was running late for her appointment with Willie. To say she was rattled is an understatement. She jumped on her cell phone to call Willie (on his house phone). When he picked up after just a few rings, she began to apologize profusely. "It's okay if you want to reschedule." In true Willie fashion, he didn't bat an eye, "I'll meet you whenever you can make it."

In August of 1927, Willie was born in the segregated Clay Street area in Shelbyville. As an African American, he will tell you that during those times, all other areas of the community were "off limits" to him. Yet, those who thought they could keep Willie out, propelled him to go even further. Willie and his friends even got permission to play tennis during the summer on the exceptionally nice concrete courts at Science Hill School, then an all-white school for girls. People would ask themselves as they watched him *go*, "How's Willie doing that?"

On those few blocks along Clay Street, Willie was raised in a family with seven kids. He went to church and attended a small school for "colored" children through ninth grade. Sometimes things happened that troubled Willie, but he never lost his ability to keep moving ahead. Willie set out to make the best of what he knew and had. He didn't let circumstances stop him from chasing his dreams. Willie had a great gift for seeing openings and making things happen.

His entrepreneurial spirit was awakened at an early age when he noticed people in his neighborhood loved fresh fish but couldn't get any. *What to do?* Open a fish market. This was his first venture to meet needs, but certainly not his last.

In 1944, segregation was still very much part of Willie's life. Injustice didn't frighten him. In order to go to high school, his only choice was The Lincoln Institute, which was created after a law passed, prohibiting students of color from attending the same school as white students. Willie knew the value of education and he was determined to keep going. He used his football and basketball talent to earn a scholarship at Fisk University in Nashville. Nashville was far from Clay Street, but Clay Street was never far from Willie. In fact, while he attended Fisk, he had friends who helped keep his fish market going.

Desegregation laws passed and news spread that the University of Louisville would begin to accept African Americans at its law school. In Willie's words, "This was a grand opportunity." When it was time for Willie to make a big move Outside, he was prepared and ready. With the help of neighbors, friends, and his savings, his dream for higher education was within reach. Willie knew that this chance was too important to waste.

Willie wouldn't be stopped from going Outside. In 1954, he and a classmate became the first African Americans to graduate from the law school. He passed the bar exam and entered the practice of law in 1955.

Amazed by his life story, I asked him, "Mr. Fleming, how did all of this change you?" With humility, Willie answered, "So many people helped me that I wanted to help others— especially my neighbors and the Clay Street community." Serving the people in his hometown became Willie's purpose. After he graduated college, he bought property that would become the area where his friends could purchase their first homes. He spent endless hours as an attorney, working on complicated deeds, wills, and trusts. Decades later, I had the privilege of negotiating the purchase of several Clay Street properties on behalf of Willie to preserve the history and memories there.

Willie's faith was always with him and still is today. He continues to care for the city, the cemeteries, and the church in his hometown. Almost ninety years old, Willie won't complain. He still rides in a carpool to his downtown Louisville office over thirty miles from home each day.

I recently walked Clay Street and saw the past come alive— the buildings, the vacant lot where the colored school once stood, the location of the fish market that provided income, the church, Willie's home. During that walk, I envisioned all that Willie accomplished and realized how easy it would have been to say, "I just can't do it."

Outsiders get over their fears and reluctance to get started. They seize opportunity. While others might run from people with problems, Outsiders run *to* them. Outsiders sit on the edge of their seats. They get fired up to see life rejuvenated. They love the story.

Outsiders work hard and develop persistence and resiliency.

They are instinctive. Outsiders are both extroverts and introverts. They are fun to be around, most of the time—well, until they start casting vision again (and again). Outsiders test their own motives and allow themselves to be changed along the way. Outsiders know what they believe and why they believe it. They know not all adventures end with great success, but they have found a way to grow despite failure and deal with the outcomes. When Outsiders fail, they identify the problem, admit the mistake, and fix it quickly. Outsiders are constantly trying things that don't make sense at first. They won't let their chance slip by. Outsiders act as spark plugs that ignite their city's engine to *go*. They are catalysts for change. Outsiders have faith and don't remain Outside of God's ways.

Willie uses actions, not just words, to inspire others to get started in their God-given calling. That's what makes Willie Fleming a true Outsider. His life exclaims, "It can be done!" He never said "I can't go there or try that," but rather, "Look what we can do."

We've all heard the stories of those who ventured out. You know, those people who quit their jobs and open businesses, the battered wife who seeks a safe haven for her children, the family who adopts an older child, people who give generously over and over, the ones who allow homeless people to stay under their roof, the executive who leaves her lucrative career to be a missionary overseas or the addict who makes the decision to stay sober for one more day. The portrait of an Outsider can look different depending on the vision, but there are a few things that they all have in common:

Outsiders look past profits to people. One couple who loved their small town, Ben and Melinda Hardin, started Harvest Coffee & Café in the front of an antique store along the town's main thoroughfare. With hearts for the community and serving farm-to-table meals, they boldly asked, "What if someone wants to eat healthy, but doesn't have the money to do so? What if once a week, we offered, Pay What You Can Day?"

Some pay little or nothing on those days, but the crazier part is that some of their customers actually pay more than their meal normally costs. The café has been featured in numerous media outlets for promoting healthy eating and community service.

Outsiders don't let their previous mistakes stop them. Reverend Charles Ashby has been through many ups and downs. He even spent three years in jail. The irony is that the cell that was created to confine him, would open his eyes to the freedom that he had in Christ. He left jail with a determination to change. He moved forward each day. Charles started recreation leagues, became the chairman of a non-profit board, initiated a much needed cab company for those without transportation, and he currently pastors a church. Charles says, "I don't love people to death, I love them to life."

Outsiders don't let their personal tragedies keep them from pushing ahead. In 2005, Ben Medley dove into a swimming pool and instantly became a quadriplegic. This hasn't stopped him. Ben refuses to stay on the side lines. After recovering, he pushed ahead in his small business. His truck and equipment are fully equipped for him to handle a lawn business with seventy yards a week. As a

> *"I can do all things through him who strengthens me."*
> *Philippians 4:13*

hard worker with tremendous persistence, Ben takes advantage of the winter by doing rehab during the off season. Then, it's back to serving his clients. He says, "Don't be afraid of your limitation, there's always adaptions. If you can't find a way to get it done, God definitely will." Ben's not done yet. His motto is: When you're not growing, you've died. While many people quote scripture, as an Outsider, Ben actually lives it.

Outsiders don't stop GOING. God put a passion inside Jeff Bracken for the poverty stricken neighborhoods of Philadelphia. Amazing things happened when Jeff stepped out in total faith and drove to the inner city from Lexington, Kentucky—

just to serve people. He used basketball to build relationships on the courts and gave the players free Gatorade. That's all he started with and that's all it took. The ministry boomed. In these neighborhoods filled with criminal activity, the residents noticed his sincerity. They'd often tell him, "Man, you crazy."

Life was going great, but then several years later Jeff was diagnosed with a rare genetic mutation called Usher Syndrome, a leading cause of becoming deaf and blind. It would have made sense for Jeff to stop going, but Jeff said, "I delight in the fact that God created a 'uniqueness' in me to be used as his vessel. In physical activity, sure Usher has

> "All the world is full of suffering.
> It is also full of overcoming."
> – Helen Keller

set me back, but what's that to me? Life isn't about me. In what really matters, Usher has propelled me forward." Jeff and his wife Mary keep going.

Jeff is now a leading teacher in his local public school system and continues to go to Philly. He has multiplied his mission and many others are engaged in serving the city now. It's beyond Jeff. Lives continue to be changed. People around Jeff have learned through his example what it means to go Outside.

"By this we know love, that he laid down his life for us, and we ought to lay down our lives for the brothers. But if anyone has the world's goods and sees his brother in need, yet closes his heart against him, how does God's love abide in him? Little children, let us not love in word or talk but in deed and in truth" (1 John 3:16-18).

Many of us are intimidated by these brave souls who have thrived outside the walls. We see the energy, the flexibility, the big vision—but we just can't seem to get there. We take one step, and it feels like a million more remain in front of us. So what do we do? We retreat. And we convince ourselves it's just better that way. We feel comfy, but in our soul we know we're coming up short. We know safety doesn't lead to significance and deep down we're miserable. Say it with me:

"There just has to be more to life!"

There is plenty of adventure to be had in the world— and it's not just reserved for a select few. Momentous things happen when ordinary people do something seemingly small. I believe everyday people like me and you can experience the thrill and reward of going Outside when we are willing to face our own feelings of insufficiency.

As we peer out the window, we see the raging storms and mountainous terrain— how could it be made easier out there? Jesus takes an opportunity to teach the disciples (and us) how our sense of inadequacy is found completely adequate in Him.

"When the apostles returned, they reported to Jesus what they had done. Then he took them with him and they withdrew by themselves to a town called Bethsaida, but the crowds learned about it and followed him. He welcomed them and spoke to them about the king-

> *"All we have to decide is what to do with the time that is given to us."*
> *— JRR Tolkien*

dom of God, and healed those who needed healing. Late in the afternoon the Twelve came to him and said, 'Send the crowd away so they can go to the surrounding villages and countryside and find food and lodging, because we are in a remote place here.' He replied, 'You give them something to eat.'

They answered, 'We have only five loaves of bread and two fish— unless we go and buy food for all this crowd.' (About five thousand men were there.) But he said to his disciples, 'Have them sit down in groups of about fifty each.' The disciples did so, and everyone sat down. Taking the five loaves and the two fish and looking up to heaven, he gave thanks and broke them. Then he gave them to the disciples to distribute to the people. They all ate and were satisfied, and the disciples picked up twelve basketfuls of broken pieces that were left over" (Luke 9:10-17 NIV).

The lesson the disciples learned when Jesus feed the 5,000 with only five loaves of bread and two fish, was that somehow our flaws and faults don't seem as big on the outside as they did when we viewed them from the inside. As Outsiders we have the distinctive chance to do something really *out there*. Not beholden to the rational and methods of the past, we have the freedom to try something new. As Jesus followers, are we willing to trust God with our inadequacy? It could be the difference between being an Outsider, or not.

"Insanity: doing the same thing over and over again and expecting different results."
– Albert Einstein

TAKE ACTION

- Read Luke 10:25-37. Who is the Outsider in this passage? What should be your motivation in becoming an Outsider?
- Name some Outsiders you've known personally or throughout history. What makes them Outsiders?
- Could you see yourself becoming an Outsider, risking something to be part of the bigger story God is writing?
- Just because someone is out front doesn't mean they are leading. Anybody can start something, but what would it look like if that something goes on beyond you?

MAHER-SHALAL-HASH-BAZ

Although the cover was dusty in seasons of my life, growing up in the South meant I always had my Bible close. But, close didn't mean I knew what it meant or how to apply in my life. In college, there was an atheist who lived across the hall from me, and he loved to slam the Bible. He would go on and on about how ridiculous it was. One day, I'd had enough and was determined to prove him wrong. I dug out my Bible, dusted it off quickly and said, "Look, the Bible is great because every time I turn to it, it has answers for me. I confidently went on, "Watch, I'll just randomly turn to any page and it will speak words to us to help us." I turned the page to an Old Testament passage: *"The Lord said to me, " 'Take a large scroll and write on it with an ordinary pen: Maher-Shalal-Hash-Baz'"* (Isaiah 8:1 NIV).

You know, Maher-Shalal-Hash-Baz. That name everyone turns to first and the longest word in the Bible! I was somehow expecting to magically impress him, but I couldn't even pronounce the name. Not surprisingly, he laughed hysterically and replied, "What a joke!" Randomly flipping through the Bible to find immediate application can certainly work, but most other times it will be super confusing—as in my case.

As I have learned to read my Bible, I've committed myself more deeply to it. The Bible is without error, the inspired and the authoritative Word of God. The text continually enriches me, grounds me, and helps me grow. These days, I just can't read it enough.

The Old and New Testament work perfectly together and the thread running right through it is found in Jesus. Take Maher-Shalal-Hash-Baz for example. On the same page as that hard-to-pro-nounce-name in my Bible, there is a fundamental

> "Jesus said, 'It is written, Man shall not live by bread alone, but by every word that comes from the mouth of God.'"
> Matthew 4:4

prophesy about a child who would change the world.

"Therefore the Lord himself will give you a sign: The virgin will conceive and give birth to a son, and will call him Immanuel" (Isaiah 7:14 NIV).

You may have heard this during a Christmas service at a local church. Why is it important? We find out later on in the New Testament, in the more familiar gospel of Matthew, the text is foretelling of the final fulfillment of the virgin birth of Jesus—the promised Messiah.

"All this took place to fulfill what the Lord had said through the prophet: 'The virgin will conceive and give birth to a son, and they will call him Immanuel' (which means 'God with us')" (Matthew 1:22-23 NIV).

It's preposterous to think about the fact that this earth-shattering prediction was nestled right on the same page that provided entertainment for my dorm-mate. Perhaps we don't understand what is right in front of us.

In the beginning, I knew the scriptures were important because someone had told me, but I never learned them for myself. I was in trouble. I couldn't explain what I believed or why I did. Fortunately, I had some friends who knew the Bible. They allowed me to ask honest questions—the hard ones, the ones people like to avoid. My life began to change.

"Therefore, if anyone is in Christ, he is a new creation. The old has

passed away; behold, the new has come" (2 Corinthians 5:17).

I have complete confidence and trust in the Bible. Especially as it relates to being an Outsider.

Many people might ask: Why do I need to consider the Bible? Why not just download the latest self-help manual? Is the Bible even relevant today? What is truth? Most of all, why is it important when it comes to me starting something?

I'm not sure what convinced me of my belief. Was it the manuscript and archaeological evidence? Eyewitness or corroborating accounts? The consistency and trustworthiness found over the course of all history in the Bible? Or, maybe just the experiences I've had with the living Word of God? I really can't point to one reason.

"In regards to this great Book (the Bible), I have but to say it is the best gift God has given to man. All the good the Savior gave to the world was communicated through this Book. But for it we could not know right from wrong. All things most desirable for man's welfare, here and hereafter, are found portrayed in it."
– Abraham Lincoln

This foundation in God's word gave me wisdom for life. As I began to explore new business ideas or opportunities to make a difference in my community, I turned to the text. Now when I need direction, I start there and keep going back. Many times, I'll still lose my way—then I realize I haven't visited my Bible recently enough.

Even if you don't believe in the message of the Bible, this fact can't be ignored: The paramount of all movements ever started, sustained, and still going, is found in the Bible and in the life of Jesus—the central figure in all of history and time.

"I am an historian, I am not a believer, but I must confess as a historian that this penniless preacher from Nazareth is irrevocably the very center of history. Jesus Christ is easily the most dominant figure in all history."
— H.G. Wells

Driving home from the beach is always the worst. Who wants to leave? *No one!* I decided a few years back that our family would take the scenic route back from Florida to Kentucky. I knew some of the back roads and thought we could find some new and interesting places to break up the monotony. Word of caution: When you go off the grid, have a full tank of gas (I didn't) and make sure you are prepared to have no cell phone reception (I wasn't).

Everyone fell asleep as soon as we hit the back hills. Beads of sweat started to form on my forehead when I noticed the gas light blink on. I tried to distract myself while singing aloud, "to grandma's house we go!" Eyes dead set on the horizon. *Surely, there will be a gas station soon.* Nothing. A few more miles. Nothing. One more mile. Nothing. Dude, things were getting super serious in a hurry. I looked over at Rachel who was peacefully sound asleep and trusting of my navigation skills. (Or, she was exhausted—pretty sure she was exhausted.)

What to do?! I felt the beginning stages of an anxiety attack forming in my chest. I swallowed my pride and woke her up to deliver the exciting news that we would be hitchhiking with our small children on the side of the road very soon. She wasn't pleased. But she did share one sliver of hope. This wasn't 1980, but for some reason she had stored a map of the states we were driving in the glove compartment.

In desperation, she found our location and, after a few quick turns, we headed towards a teeny town that probably had a population of forty-two people. We cut the air conditioning and started praying hard. Real hard.

Coming over a ridge, I saw life. A farmer! I pulled aside, "Mr. Farmer man, how much further to a gas station?"

He said, "What in the he_ _ are you doing out here, son?"

I almost kicked him off the tractor and siphoned all his gas, but I just replied, "Yes sir, I'm lost and it's not proper leadership befalling a husband and father of three."

"Welp," he said, "you're a lucky _____."

He dug his finger in our map, "Right there. You'll find a filling station about three miles up ahead." I thanked him and gave him a bar of soap for his dirty mouth— especially in front of my kids.

We rolled up to the dilapidated station to find a man smoking right in front of the only pump. "They must be out of business." I groaned and dropped my head on the steering wheel. That's when the man (an employee, apparently) motioned us on in to fill up. Unbelievable. If Rachel hadn't brought the old school maps, we would have been staying the night under a Spanish moss tree surrounded by the howls of coyotes.

Outsiders must take a field guide as well, and that guide is the Bible. When an Outsider begins to examine and think on the Bible, they must not read as if it's all about their desires and dreams. This guide is not "me" focused, its Christ focused. Of

> Your word is a lamp to my feet and a light to my path.
> Psalm 119:105

course, that means the direction the Outsider wants to take might not be the path God is calling them to take. In fact, there will be many that won't understand or desire to take the field guide's instructions.

"Don't look for shortcuts to God. The market is flooded with surefire, easygoing formulas for a successful life that can be practiced in your spare time. Don't fall for that stuff, even though crowds of people do. The way to life—to God!—is vigorous and requires total attention (Matthew

7:13-14 MSG).

Here's the thing. Outsiders are wired to explore and go off the typical route. Our adventures often lead us into uncertain territory. Sometimes we get lost and run out of gas. We start to second guess our decisions. We are desperate for direction. Long before that moment of distress, we can turn to the Bible to give us the big picture and the information that we need to refuel and catch our bearings.

"The only place we can find a clear, unmistakable message is in the Word of God."
– Billy Graham

TAKE ACTION

- Buy a study Bible. I use the ESV Study Bible. http://esvstudybible.org/
- Pick a theme or a specific book to study. As an example, read the Book of Acts and follow as the Church got its start. Watch the movement unfold. Ask others to read with you. Take notes.
- As scripture speaks to you, print it out, send it to your inbox, or make it the wallpaper on your phone. Just get it to a place where you will see it every day. Do this throughout your journey.

Element
Two:
Vision

"...so Jesus also suffered *outside* the gate in order to sanctify the people through his own blood..."

QUESTIONABLE FOOT-WASHING

Sometimes the answers you need to get started can be found in the right question.

In 2005, Rachel and I became friends with Kristy Barrett. Kristy has cerebral palsy. At that time, I didn't have any friends who were wheelchair bound. I certainly didn't know anyone dealing with daily pain like she endures.

One day Kristy told me that she had something to share with me and Rachel. "I want to wash your feet."

What? I felt awkward and unsure. *Another girl besides Rachel wanted to wash my feet? I'm pretty sure Rachel wouldn't even want to wash my feet. What if they smell? I don't think I've cared for my toenails in years. Besides, how would Kristy wash my feet? She needed help getting her own shoes on by herself.*

"Why?" I asked.

She simply said, "God told me to do it." Needless to say, that was a life changing moment. Kristy just wanted to follow the example of Jesus.

Jesus knew that the Father had put him in complete charge of everything, that he came from God and was on his way back to God. So he got up from the supper table, set aside his robe, and put on an apron. Then he poured water into a basin and began to wash the feet of the disciples, drying them with his apron. When he got to Simon Peter, Peter said, "Master, you wash my feet?"

Then he said, *"Do you understand what I have done to you? You address me as 'Teacher' and 'Master,' and rightly so. That is what I am. So if I, the Master and Teacher, washed your feet, you must now wash each other's feet. I've laid down a pattern for you. What I've done, you do. I'm only pointing out the obvious. A servant is not ranked above his master; an employee doesn't give orders to the employer. If you understand what I'm telling you, act like it—and live a blessed life"* (John 13: 12-17 MSG).

Christ Jesus washed his friends' feet as a final proof of love for them. He set an example of humility. In fact, Jesus washed the feet of all of his disciples, even Judas, the one he knew was going to betray him.

Kristy's life modeled servant leadership for me. It wasn't snazzy or well-oiled, but her presence spoke a question that would be burned into our hearts: "How can I serve you?"

Robert A. Raines summed up this perspective in his book, "Creative Brooding," when he wrote:

> *Lord, I size up other people in terms of what they can do for me: How they can further my program, feed my ego, satisfy my needs, give me strategic advantage. I exploit people ostensibly for Your sake, but really for my own sake.*
>
> *Lord, I have often turned to You to get the inside track for special favors, direction for my schemes, power for my projects, sanction for my ambitions, a blank check for whatever I want. Change me, Lord. Make me a person who asks of You, and asks of others, 'What can I do for you?'*

Questions not answers. Outsiders learn that questions are better than answers. What's so wrong with asking questions any-way? When I started thinking Outside of the norm, I felt like I needed to have all the answers. It was exhausting. As I watched other servant leaders, they asked lots of questions. They didn't act like they knew what people were talking about all the time.

Kristy taught me that if I really wanted to serve others, I had to recognize that I needed help too. The foot washing humbled me. Once I realized that going Outside meant I didn't have to have all the answers and it wasn't about me, my mind soared with possibilities of what might be. What a R-E-L-I-E-F. An Outsider develops an exploratory mentality and gives themselves permission to journey with more questions than answers. This approach is a healthy sign, because the quicker an Outsider can acknowledge that they are not *all-knowing*, they will turn to the One who is.

Rachel and I agreed to participate in the foot washing session with Kristy. I know some of you are thinking that's a very strange thing to do. Well, for me it was super important. Not only did it teach me about Christ-centered servanthood, but it would also give me the temperament I needed when Rachel and I got married.

It was a snowy and cold day when Rachel and I went on our first date. Trying to impress with a simplistic, yet romantic approach, I had the idea of going on a walk in our city park. She agreed and we bundled up and headed outside. As we strolled under the heavy-laden tree canopies and threw snowballs at each other, I forgot how cold it was.

It was time for me to test the feelings out, discover if any mutuality existed. So, I stopped on the snowy path and formed a heart in the snow with my boot. She crossed it out and drew a smiley face as if to say, "I just want to be friends." Dang. But, I knew by the way she threw the snow in my face and laughed, that friends didn't do that to each other. She either was going to love me forever or ditch me on the way home.

Fortunately, Rachel gave me more opportunities to turn the smiley face into a heart. We dated and it became obvious that we really were in love and that God was calling us together. I bought a ring and invited Rachel back to that same park for another walk. It was a beautiful summer day, but she was not expecting my proposal when we approached a park bench that just so happened to have a small pale of water, washcloth, and soap underneath. (How'd that get there!?) I got down on my knees and asked her to marry me. She said, "Of Course!" (That was one question I had to have the answer for!)

As I took the foot-washing gear out and washed her feet, we could hear the nearby water streaming and birds singing. I thought, "God, you really do have my back!" Since we've been married now for over ten years, it's been helpful to recall an early foundation of service and humility towards each other. We've had lots of questions we didn't know the answers for, but together we've trusted a God who continues to be abundantly faithful.

"A healthy outside starts from the inside."
– Robert Urich

TAKE ACTION

- Make a list of questions you need to get answered before you start.
- Share a meal with friends. Ask them your questions. Listen to their answers.
- List the ways your vision can help meet the needs of others.

PONYBOY AND THE "IN CROWD"

Marti Brown couldn't stand it. The evening she met a group of urban kids who had been dropped off at her church would forever change her. These children were struggling, had many needs, and little hope. They needed a refuge—a place to be. For many people this problem was just that: A problem. But to Marti it was an opportunity to join the action and to love all kids—no matter where they came from or who they were.

Twenty years later, Marti and her ministry, Father's Love, continue to serve the community. It's simple, Marti and her team love kids like Jesus does. She provides them with a safe environment, educates them about character values and nutrition, prays earnestly for each of them and the generational cycles they battle and teaches them from the Bible. She and her team also help the kids learn practical skills like sewing and reading, and organizes fun activities like puppet shows.

One of the kids that benefited from Marti's care was the young Rachel (not-yet) Webb. When my wife was only nine years old, her parents divorced and stopped going to church. That's when Marti, Rachel's former elementary teacher who lovingly referred to her as "Rachelini Fettucini with a Pizza on Her Head," stepped in and drove her to church every Sunday and every Wednesday. Rachel and all the kids Marti ministered may have had many needs, but more than anything, Marti would give them a place to fit in.

In the novel, *The Outsiders*, Ponyboy and his gang, the Greasers, had a rival gang called the Socs, short for Socials. Their hatred for each other was palpable. The Greasers were from the poor side of town and the Socs were the rich kids from the other side. In the story, we learn the "in" crowd can't stand those on the "out," and the Outside crowd is happy to reciprocate when given the chance.

> *"They grew up on the outside of society. They weren't looking for a fight. They were looking to belong."*
> — S.E. Hinton

After interactions between the Greasers and Socs elevate, and a death of one of the Socs occurs, Ponyboy and another Greaser, Johnny, are forced to find a hideout. Ironically, a rural church serves as the place where they truly take on the persona of being society's Outsiders. Ponyboy and his friends didn't fit the mold. They lived in preconceived boxes and were trying to do their best to get out of them. Taking matters into their own hands only worsened their situation. But did they really want all this drama?

As the novel continues, the drama thickens until the conclusion. A fire leaves children stranded in the church where Ponyboy and Johnny have been hiding. They rush to help and Johnny ends up sacrificing his life to save the children. On Johnny's deathbed, he tells Ponyboy to "Stay Gold," which is in reference to the poem Ponyboy had recited earlier to Johnny as they looked outside at the golden sky.[1]

"Nature's first green is gold
Her hardest hue to hold.
Her early leaf's a flower;
But only so an hour.
Then leaf subsides to leaf.

So Eden sank to grief,
So dawn goes down to day.
Nothing gold can stay."[2]

Johnny's encouragement to Ponyboy was to stay set apart. But how do we "stay gold"? Is possible that we can be pure within ourselves or have the desire to help others strive towards the same? Is it even worth trying?

"Once you were alienated from God and were enemies in your minds because of your evil behavior. But now he has reconciled you by Christ's physical body through death to present you holy in his sight, without blemish and free from accusation" (Colossians 1:21-22 NIV).

Before Christ, a priest would bring unblemished sacrifices to God as an attempt to reconcile our estrangement from God. Now, as believers in Jesus, we can stop "trying on our own" and recognize that Jesus is the One who makes us without stain. God is the only one who provides the answer and compels us to care for those on the Outside. Johnny's death reminds us that those who are vulnerable need help and in the end, that includes all of us. To be an Outsider, we must recognize the need all of us have for belonging. Not just for ourselves, but for our neighbors too. Outsiders run to those Outside and do their best to welcome them in—to show those on the "out," the love of God.

In most communities there are people living on the fringe. What separates them from the rest of us could be a railroad track, a broken down fence, or a two lane road. As I became more and more aware of this personally, I had to explore it further. I wanted to know why these barriers existed. I'm still learning and have lots more to go, but I quickly found out that getting in the game and simple interaction was a great start. For years, I had driven by countless non-profits, food pantries, and shelters, and if I kept moving fast enough I could keep my conscience clear. Wasn't I busy enough trying to provide for my family and maintaining payroll? Wasn't attending church regularly and coaching youth soccer enough?

Until one day I pulled over. I got out of the car and it felt totally bizarre. *What was I doing? Is this safe? What will these people think of me?* As if I knew where I was, I walked through the door of one of those shelters, and there I saw Judy Roberts. She was scurrying around from room to room, running the cash register, helping people find the right size of clothing, counseling ladies, and answering the phone. I got the overwhelming sense there was much more happening then my drive-by judgment. I asked Judy, "What's going on in here?" She was a little surprised that someone would ask and frankly I was very surprised that I was the one asking. Immediately my mind raced. *I hope she doesn't ask me to do something.* As to my question, Judy calmly replied, "I'm here doing God's work and honestly, I didn't think I would ever be here." That transparency leveled the playing field of my thinking immediately. Judy showed me that an Outsider wasn't comfortable even after they took the first step Outside. Maybe I wasn't the only one who felt out of place?

My stereotypical assumptions were lost in the relationships I was forming with Judy and other everyday people serving those on the Outside. I'd always felt like I was on the "inside," but now I understood how bad it felt to be on the Outside—it stinks. My heart wanted to join the people there. Instead of associating with others because of my personal assets and belongings, I started to associate with others because we all shared the need to belong.

True Outsiders are, first, broken people themselves. Outsiders know Jesus has given them a place to belong and has set them free to go Outside to people who are broken and are trying to find their way "in" as well. Outsiders like Marti and Judy, usually don't have to look very far to recognize God is leading us to meet a need that is standing right in front of us.

If you look for truth, you may find comfort in the end: if you look for comfort you will not get either comfort or truth—only soft soap and wishful thinking to begin with and, in the end, despair.
- C.S. Lewis

TAKE ACTION

- What weaknesses do you need to account for before you go Outside?
- What boxes have you created in your own mind to keep you from going Outside?
- Have you been waiting to "feel" ready to *go*? If so, have you considered applying the necessary faith to go Outside?
- Have you given yourself the space to count the costs of going and then humbly say "Yes" to God?
- Are you willing to . . .
  - o Trust in Jesus and His love before ever trying to go out on your own?
  - o Step out into the fringe, even if it feels weird?
  - o Involve yourself in finding out more about those who are on the Outside of society?
  - o Learn the names of others that don't look or dress like you?
  - o Count the costs, make the sacrifice?

Welcome to Whoville

As I sat alone at the round table in my real estate office, I was confused. I had been working tirelessly with an organization I cared deeply about, to help them find a new location. This non-profit provided food and clothing to those that need it, was growing, and had a donor that was willing to give a significant amount of money to buy property. In the real estate world, if an entity has a great track record, is expanding, has plenty of money, and *can't* find a location, you must not have the right agent—or at least that's what I thought looking in my imaginary mirror.

Growing tired of searching online databases, I had to get out of the office. So, I started walking the streets and began to pray. I tried hard to see the community I had been looking at for decades, with fresh eyes. Still nothing. I asked myself a number of questions. *What if we build something? What if we combined two buildings? What if something old was revitalized?*

I kept on walking, looking up at the old, cold, brick structures. I even peered off into the area outside of downtown and imagined the perfect facility sitting on a hillside with four board fences surrounding it. In these moments of desperation, it was time for a coffee. Without a moment's hesitation, I stepped inside for a jolt and made my way back out to a bench on Main

Street. I sat there looking and shrugging at the broken sidewalk. Then, I noticed something.

People's feet.

I'd been focused on the building, not the mission. This organization's purpose had always been fueled by people not buildings. In fact, their previous location was a disaster. It was disorganized and small, but the amount of love shared in that dated and inefficient space made it seem like a suburban Class A professional building.

It was like I had forgotten the heart of God. In His loving way, He wanted to use this experience for much more than a single transaction.

So, in our next meeting as I was talking with one of the organization's directors, they randomly told me about a building that people had been walking and praying over. It was a much larger building that needed a lot of TLC and elbow grease. Many of these praying people had no idea what it could be used for specifically, but were hoping that it would be used for God's purposes.

I started thinking about the organization I was working for and thought, maybe, just maybe. It was near the center of town and was easily accessible by lots and lots of people who needed their services. Ah yes, people. There it was.

The reasons the building wouldn't work physically, like the leaky roof, vastness of size, the apparent disintegration of the façade, and intimidating cost might be overcome. In a matter of seconds, the opportunity was unveiled. It was suddenly perfect.

For the next ten months we worked vigorously to make the dream a reality. By God's grace, we were able to move through all the ups and downs of due diligence and the many hurdles that arose. The building was finally purchased and operates today as a place of grace.

As a commercial real estate broker, it's hard telling how many times someone has called me with a new idea for a business or non-profit. It starts for folks in a multitude of ways. Maybe it's a fresh dream, an anticipated need, or it's born out of employer thwarting a good notion. Newly appointed entrepreneurs usually toss around some ideas a bit, and quickly move to putting their energy into finding a location.

I'm always happy to take new calls and leads! But when they call me first, they've started with the wrong person. I'm the guy marketing the location. I'm the "where" guy. All too often in a hurriedly fashion, perceived starters move quickly to "Where could it go?" or "Tell ya what, this would be a great location for (insert idea here)."

This is a wrong approach for Outsiders. Going Outside is all about the "who," not the "where." In the beginning, the "where" isn't important. In fact, an early focus on the "where" can stop a movement. Slow down and take this in:

The "who" drives the "where" and the "where" should never drive the "who."

This is an important distinction.

The "where" is the easy way. The "where" is often a study of science. It promotes logic and critical thinking. These aren't bad things, but too much energy on the "where" takes an Outsider down the wrong path. The "where" is never enough for an Outsider, because a true Outsider is driven by the "who." However, the problem that we often face is that the organic nature of the "who" can be a little messy and hard to fit in that perfect "where" box. An insider will say, "If we make the "where" awesome and program it effectively, the 'who' will take care of itself." Nope. This approach might have worked in the past, but Outsiders must focus on the future.

For years, many of us knew that men were living under a bridge in our town. Although some people tried to help them, there didn't seem to be a permanent solution. That is until a local church pastor, Lee Bean, showed up. For Lee and a few of his concerned church members, they couldn't stand the thought of men living in such horrific conditions. Lee wondered if they had ever been offered any solid, consistent, or tangible help.

Lee and some friends decided to reach out to these men. They started by getting to know their names and establishing the "who." They became friends with them. They found out how to best help each one. They gave them hope. These efforts led to local men's homeless ministry named the Open Door of Hope. When it all started, Lee and his team didn't know "how" they would minister to these men and certainly didn't have the "where" planned out. The Open Door of Hope wasn't driven by a location. As the ministry developed, and the emphasis and commitment to these men was established, this expression of hope finally became a "where" and the organization would have a "where" to serve from and are still expanding today.

We continually serve a generation that won't be fooled because the "where" is perfect. Millennials and others ask questions like, "How are you making a difference in what you do? How are you caring for people and the environment through your activities? Is this healthy? Is this idea authentic in doing what is right for others?"

Early in his ministry, Jesus was ministering at the synagogues, a place where lots of perceived Insiders hang out. Jesus, being the leader of the ultimate Outside movement, headed to a lake, where he engaged with some fishermen. These ordinary and untrained men would be his first true followers.

Jesus boarded Simon's boat and told him to let down his nets for a catch. Simon replied, *"Master, we toiled all night and took nothing! But at your word I will let down the nets." And when they had done this, they enclosed a large number of fish, and their nets were breaking. They signaled to their partners in the other boat to come and help. And they came and filled both the boats, so that they began to sink. Simon saw it, he fell down at Jesus' knees, saying, "Depart from me, for I am a sinful man, O Lord." For he and all who were with him were astonished . . . And Jesus said to Simon, "Do not be afraid; from now on you will be catching men." And when they had brought their boats to land, they left everything and followed him"* (Luke 5:5-11).

Jesus taught these ordinary fishermen to stop focusing on the fish, or the "what." He introduced the idea of centering our activities on the "who." We need to be fishers of people, not fishers of fish. The focus on the "who" caused these early followers to pursue what was central. They turned towards the "who" and stepped out. In fact, they didn't even ask about the "how." They left everything and headed Outside.

I still walk by the beautiful brick building where the non-profit operates and even now, I try not to look at the structure. I'll sit on the stone wall across the street and take a deep breath. It's a perfect spot to watch the feet of people going in and out. I see the amount of time, energy, passion, and people that make the organization successfully provide for others.

The "who" were giving and the "who" were finding what they needed—the love of Jesus.

TAKE ACTION

- Identify the "who" in your vision? Get specific. Make a list.

- Determine from this list people you'll need to have coffee with or learn from this week. Set it up. Make it happen.

- What did you learn? Record that. How has what you learned developed your strategy for your future "where" or "what"?

- As you allow the "who" to drive your process, start formulating the needs of the "where" and the "what."

THE DREAM OF THE NINETIES IS ALIVE IN SHELBYVILLE

Late one evening, I was hoping to plow through some writing on a tight deadline, and in these moments of creative weakness, it's often hard to find guidance. So, after putting the kids to bed and boxing up Legos so I didn't step on them later, I sat down at the kitchen table, pen in hand.

All my imaginative ability was slipping away as I tried to envision myself in a log cabin with a real fireplace, instead of the fake gas logs that don't work in my house. Not giving up, I brewed some bad tea and lit three candles to generate the perfect ambiance for killer creativity—but still nothing.

Time was moving on and as I stared at the dirty dishes, my feelings shifted to sheer desperation. In distressing times, well, you take distressing measures. For me, that's 90s grunge music. Although it's awkward ground to cover that is highly unpredictable, it always somehow induces productivity. Like a bolt of lightning, Eddie Vedder jarred me with his powerful baritone voice in the background. Time stopped. I went to my closet and got my oversized flannel shirt and tied it around my waist. Problem solved. I was back in the groove. For some reason, the lyrics in the song caused me to reflect on scripture and the impact the gospel has on people. The vision came soaring back to me in ways that I hadn't ever dreamed it could.

So what's the point? If you're up for a random story, am I

up for sharing one?

Hmm. Probably. But, actually, the point is that there is something remarkable about a God-given vision. It chases after you. It shows up everywhere and in everything. Some might refer to this as a frequency illusion or another phenomenon of sorts. In reality, it's much bigger.

Most of us know the story of Jonah. Maybe you recall that God called Jonah to go share His love with the people Jonah didn't like. Jonah thought he could outrun God and got on a boat. The sea became turbulent and Jonah told the others on board it was his fault. These men were very afraid. They said to Jonah:

"What have you done. . .What should we do to you to make the sea calm down for us?" (Jonah 1:10-11 NIV).

Jonah told them to throw him into the sea. But what happens next is interesting. The men didn't automatically hurl in him the water. I probably would have! No, they actually rowed hard to get back to dry land (Jonah 1:13). But these men too, found out what Jonah had finally submitted himself to understand: When God gives a specific vision and task, you can run but you can't hide. You can row harder and harder, but you won't get anywhere. In the end, they tell Jonah sorry and hurl him into the sea. God rescues Jonah through the belly of a whale and Jonah goes where God is calling him.

"Vision is the art of seeing what is invisible to others."
– Jonathan Swift

As always, God's ways are higher than ours.

Leaders who have vision become Outsiders when they finally understand that the vision they have is not for them. That God gives vision for His glory not ours—and that's a good thing! We learn like Jonah did, that God's vision He provides is not to harm us, but for us to experience His love. As the vision shows up in everything and everywhere, it's God showing us that He still cares and He has a purpose. How reassuring!

I praise you, for I am fearfully and
wonderfully made.
Wonderful are your works;
my soul knows it very well.
My frame was not hidden from you,
when I was being made in secret,
intricately woven in the depths of the earth.
Your eyes saw my unformed substance;
in your book were written, every one of them,
the days that were formed for me,
when as yet there was none of them.
How precious to me are your thoughts, O God!
How vast is the sum of them!
Psalm 139:14-17

For the Outsider, allowing God's purpose to flow through you is a key to establishing a vision. And, vision is essential. Going Outside creates enough questions and plenty of uncertainty. Lacking forward-thinking and a clarity of calling will make it tough when you get chastised—and you will.

There are many methods that can be used to cultivate and articulate a vision. In addition, there have been countless resources devoted to helping leaders develop a vision and mission statement. The Outsider has to discover their own vision and then lead it. *No one else should or can own the vision that God is giving you.*

While you work on outlining your vision and mission here's a few things we've learned that could be helpful:

- Vision is the future in-the-making. As Proverbs 29:18 says, *"Where there is no vision, the people perish."*
- Mission fuels how you'll get there.
- Good vision should be clear and simple. It always adds value.

71

- Don't rush it with vision. Developing the ability to know where God is leading can be a process. Often, days will seem like weeks and weeks like days. Don't get weighed down by timetables. Eugene Peterson said, "Hurry is a form of violence practiced on time. But time is sacred."
- Don't try to steal someone else's vision. It's not uniquely yours. Without authenticity, a vision isn't sustainable. A.W. Tozer said, "The world is waiting to hear an authentic voice, a voice from God—not an echo of what others are doing and saying, but an authentic voice."
- Don't let planning get in the way of GOING. Peter Marshall said, "Small deeds done are better than great deeds planned."
- Don't allow the operational elements drive the vision. Dream bigger.
- Get started by chasing the vision. The details and resources will come later. Be accustomed to saying, "We know we have a flight and destination, but we'll have to build the plane as we fly it—some seats will be missing, we could be low on fuel, and the wing might be damaged, but we are still going."
- Be ready to clarify the path in which you are headed. Then you'll be able to explain why you won't go other directions.
- Articulating vision promotes honesty and integrity. With an established vantage point, others can decide if they want in.
- Saying "No" will be just as important as saying "Yes."
- Protecting vision will become your job. Others are coming to circumvent, hijack, control, detour or manipulate your cause. Don't let it happen. Steward the vision and guard it.
- Vision flows from God and deepens over time. Especially after you're gone. *Say What!*
- Start to practice communicating your vision with

friends who will help you learn to speak more clearly. Get your elevator pitch ready. Practice and sharpen it to succinct form.

As my night at the kitchen table came to a close, I marveled at how I had searched so diligently for the vision that had really never left. In an instant, God opened my eyes and brought back stories about how there is much more to going Outside then I ever imagined. After all, Outside is a pretty huge place. As I arose and unknotted the flannel shirt, the dream that started for me in Shelbyville was still alive and kicking. I was just glad the music was over. Oh, and that the 90s were too.

A vision without a task makes a visionary.
A task without a vision makes for drudgery.
A vision and a task makes a missionary.
— George Deakin

TAKE ACTION

- Read the book of Nehemiah in the Old Testament. Think of your calling. Journey with Nehemiah as you process the vision.
- Put a whiteboard up somewhere you can leave it. Get the burden out of your head and on the board. Throw it all up, stay with it, mark through it, and use different colors. Get others involved.
- Keep working on a written vision. It will come as you take more steps in the process.
- Draft a 12-month starting plan. Don't allow money to alter the ideas. How much bigger would your dream be if money had nothing to do with it?

THE CASH
COW IS BULL

On a late afternoon in March, Josh, and Melissa Ballard were pretty excited about their plans for the evening. Once they had all their chores finished, they were headed off the cattle farm and out with friends. Raising kids, working, volunteering in the community and at church, and having a cattle farm made for busy lives, so this was a rare and special occurrence.

Just when the day looked done, they realized that their two baby calves were missing. They had to be found! It had become too cold and risky to leave them out. After searching frantically, they located them. One hour until their scheduled dinner, they found themselves carrying two fifty-pound calves through the muddy terrain to the barn. The mess they had become was about to ruin their night. Melissa said, "Why are we doing this? We aren't even making money and here we are trudging through the nasty, cold hillside for what?!

Josh and Melissa started in the cattle business with a handful of cows at his father's farm. Josh had a passion for being on the farm and it was a fun way to stay connected to his passion. Then he bought his father's herd of cattle. It seemed that this might be something worth pursuing, so they had to find a closer farm. Farmland was hard to locate, but after patiently looking over a period of time, a spot opened up.

Their philosophy in the business was simple. Reinvest the proceeds they would make into more cattle and land. Grow the business gradually over a period of time and don't hurry the process. Involve their kids in the work and make it a family affair. As opportunities come up, consider them and if it fits, take the chance!

> "A single dream is more powerful than a thousand realities."
> – J.R.R. Tolkien

This approach was the opposite of the proverbial and instant cash cow. (Pun intended.) The one that says if we just put a little money into a venture, we'll get an overflowing amount of mailbox money each week. We'll be so profitable, that we won't have to work anymore and reinvesting money won't be needed because we'll be so flush, it'll just take care of itself.

Do Outsiders need a cash cow to get started? A way to fuel their dream and make their lives easier? Is it possible that a cash cow is actually all *bull?*

As Outsiders, we can't allow finances to drive our thinking. Financial anxiety smothers opportunities that would have been real possibilities. As Outsiders, we must keep our hearts set on our calling and invite others to go Outside with us. Like Josh and Melissa, most Outsiders start small and don't get ahead of themselves. *Outsiders know that going Outside is a marathon, not a sprint.*

In the beginning you think it's all about money, but in the end, it's not about the money. In fact, money ain't "all that" anyways. It's actually ruined many visions. It's about a God who sends and equips. If the money isn't there initially keep trudging ahead. If God wills it, He is plenty able to provide in many ways:

"And God is able to bless you abundantly, so that in all things at all times, having all that you need, you will abound in every good work" (2 Corinthians 9:8).

What if I told you it was possible to have an Outsider dream that starts and grows, but never has to pay rent? Even better, what if that same dream didn't have to borrow money either? I can hear the cynics and skeptics, "This must be a hoax, what's the catch?" Maybe you have heard the one-in-a-million stories. The ones that happen to everyone else. I know what you mean; I'm usually there with you—the doubter that remains

> *The courage of one man stiffens the spine of another.*
> *– Billy Graham*

unconvinced. But, by God's grace I was able to really be a part of actually seeing financial miracles happen all because of God's provision as I began to learn that money was not the only thing I needed to feel equipped. Oddly (and sometimes frustratingly) God doesn't necessarily call the equipped but he always, without a doubt, equips the called.

Josh and Melissa made it to their farm to table dinner that night. As they exhaustedly walked into the café door, they were given a huge round of applause for their persistent commitment and efforts to bring 100% grass fed beef to the community. Melissa's question from earlier in the day was answered resoundingly. Melissa says, "I love it when people love what we do, and even better I know it's God's way of affirming our families calling to honor God with our resources while promoting a healthier lifestyle."

An Outsider's focus shouldn't be developing a cash cow. It ought to be on the vision God gives and provides for. The grind Outside is worth it.

TAKE ACTION

- Our mentors, Karl and Susan Babb were quick to remind Rachel and me that Hebrews 13 didn't end with verse 15, which is where we usually stopped. They asked us to keep reading until we arrived at verses 20-21. I'd encourage you to do the same.
- Draft a proposed budget needed to fund your Outsider

vision. Share it with interested people and invite them to help. Perhaps they can help you establish an income model based on the money they would normally spend or give to a vision such as yours.

- Read John 13:29. If Jesus put a thief in charge of the money, do you think He was concerned with money being the driving factor?

Element Three: Learning

"...Therefore let us go to him **outside** the camp and bear the reproach he endured..."

LEARNING TO UNLEARN

Have you ever driven somewhere on a sunny day and by the time you arrived, a torrential downpour started—out of nowhere? Me too, it's not fun. But this time, I saw this random occurrence as a chance to serve. As I pulled into my location's parking lot, I sat there to let the storm pass. But it wasn't.

People were getting drenched, racing from their cars to their various destinations within the building without an umbrella. This rain was a total surprise. Looking around, I found a random umbrella smashed up in the rear hatch. I'm not sure I would have ever used it for myself, but I forced it open. The pathetic little thing showed off how jilted it had become. However, I kept watching people get soaked, so I reluctantly stepped out and took what I had.

I was surprised not many people cared much about the umbrella's condition, but sincerely appreciated the help and the ability to stay somewhat dry. I got soaked, but it was so much fun. I started just giving it to people for them to carry themselves. It left me with nothing, but I had more then I needed in that moment.

People watched me as I kept going. Nobody said much, but I stayed at it. One particular friend noticed my insanity and lack of proper equipment to carry out the task. He came up to me with his super-sized canopy and said, "Here Lee, use this!" So I immediately threw the other contraption down and got going with what I really needed to do the best job. This proved

"I write for the unlearned about things in which I am unlearned myself."
– C.S. Lewis

to be much more effective. When it was over, I stood looking at the washed up parking lot and wished the rain wouldn't stop!

It's pretty crazy what people will do when they see you step out in faith. They'll give you a better umbrella. Often times they will go so far to support you with your vision and opportunity, you won't even believe it!

My attempts to go Outside are overrun with the amount of people that have invested in me and helped me. Through their willingness to overlook my hang-ups and aid in my risky adventures, I have learned of God's faithfulness and equipping.

My assumption that people would really care about the appearance and condition of my umbrella almost stopped me from helping others. Heck, I also assumed that the rain itself and the idea of getting drenched would make the time spent miserable. But in fact, there I was outside in the rain, enjoying every minute.

When I was in high school, I made the varsity soccer team my freshman year. Although almost every other player was much larger in stature, I could use my skills and agility to move quickly and out maneuver other players. I had a load of stamina and endurance. We would play ninety minutes, and it wasn't a problem for me and my teammates to sprint all over the place.

Running in the game was no issue, but practice was another story. Every day after school, we'd show up at the soccer field to scrimmage and prepare for the next game. Our coach would actually drive onto the grass area in his red pickup truck, roll down his window and exclaim, "Boys, run the park." Our bellies were full from scarfing down McDonald's and our mindset was equally apathetic after sitting in class all day, but we slowly took off. Running the park was mundane, but the scenery was helpful. We'd trek along in the tall itchy grass beside a fence passing a golf course, softball fields, a nursery, baseball fields, and playgrounds. As long as we all came back fairly close together within a reasonable amount of time, we stayed out of trouble.

There was no clear or actual path, so often times we'd come up with our own version of "running the park." One day we decided there might be a more convenient route. Once we got to the nursery filled with trees, Coach couldn't see us. So we took some rest. The plan was to wait fifteen minutes and swing back around where we usually finish without having to travel the entire distance. It was solid plan, until our one teammate who loved to run the park and win every day, went off the path. This teammate knew that running was important to our success and was incredibly focused on becoming better. He wouldn't settle for less.

It reminds me of the movie, *The Maze Runner*, where Thomas awakens in an unfamiliar place known as the Glade, left with no memories of his past, except his name. A gigantic maze surrounds the community of people living in the Glade. In order to learn more, the residents elect certain members to run the maze and determine what is happening on the Outside. These risk takers are elevated as "runners" and the others wait inside, anticipating the runners' findings.

Thomas is nominated to be a runner and heads into the maze with the concentration of an Outsider. Go Thomas! He joins Minho, who is the head runner and has spent many, many days searching the maze. Being new to the situation is an advantage to Thomas, but it also requires a lot of courage. Thomas isn't afraid to use his curiosity

"The world has changed. Our customers have changed. We have to change, too."
– Jim Cantalupo
Former CEO of McDonald's

and an unwillingness to conform to the status quo. He is seeking a better and preferred future.

After being in the maze with Thomas, Minho teaches us all a lesson. We find that Minho has the values of an Outsider too. He understands the importance of unlearning all that he had learned to let go of all that he personally found, in order to see a better outcome realized. Minho recognizes that Thomas' fresh perspective is eye-opening. Minho exclaims to the others, "Look, I don't know if he's (Thomas) brave or stupid. But whatever it is, we need more of it."

Thomas quickly familiarizes himself with the inside world and determines it to be a place where they will surely die. He exclaims to all the residents, "I am willing to risk a life out there rather than in here, because this place isn't our home."[3]

Even though his past is foggy, and his current reality is full of uncertainty, he strives toward a better future for himself and others and he begins to reexamine all that he has learned.

When I think of coming home, I think of a kid who has just scraped his knee and is thinking, *I'm not going to **walk** home, I'm not calling for my mom—I am in pain, I am distraught, and the only thing that will make this right is if I can **run** home.*

You just want refuge.

"For here we have no lasting city, but we seek the city that is to come." Hebrews 13:14 (NIV)

If we can get our mind right and focus on that "city that is to come" and focus less about knowing too much or not knowing enough, you are able to readjust your thinking and learn to unlearn in order to orient your thinking on the Outside. On the city that is to come. On your ultimate home. On the eternal, important, and ever-lasting things.

Outsiders take what they have learned and apply it in useful ways—they don't allow the past to be impediments for the future. The Outsider's humility to keep unlearning is critical to allowing the vision to grow as it needs. Don't box yourself in to the same methods. Your ability to unlearn will help keep the focus on moving ahead and will demonstrate to others you aren't in it for yourself. Remember, going Outside is a pioneering of new opportunities. A willingness to utilize a new scorecard. Be innovative. Hold your methods loosely as you *go*.

TAKE ACTION

- With all you've learned, perhaps you think of yourself as a trendsetter and Outsider today. But, tomorrow, will you be ready to "unlearn" for the sake of the mission? How are you preparing yourself?
- Meet with other experienced starters. Ask them about their unlearning process.
- Find others who are learning as they go. Start today by following five Outsider role models on social media. Apply the new things you learn.
- As you are learning, take time to read 2 Peter 1:5-8. Which biblical virtues can you sharpen as you prepare for your new adventure? Notice that faith is listed first and love is last.

WALLPAPER BORDER AND LAVENDER PAINT

It was bad.

As we walked into the house my mouth dropped to the floor. Wallpaper. Border.

Winnie the Pooh, seashells, nature views, and Snow White and the seven dwarfs, to name a few—the imagery was unpredictable and daunting. I detest wallpaper border for many reasons, but mostly because it is notoriously difficult to remove. These playful designs looked like they had been up for years. The old plaster behind each design silently whispered, "You're not taking my borders off." Forget a hair dryer, spray bottle, or pocket-scraper; we needed an industrial power washer.

As if the wallpaper border was bad enough, more than half the house was painted lavender. Not an elegant and soft purple, but a raging 1980's purple. One of the team members walked in and said, "Do we have any primer? Do we have enough paint for two or three coats?"

It was so bad. *Chip and Joanna Gaines, we need you!* A week before, looking at the outside of the small house, I told the non-profit director, "We'll have this knocked out in a weekend." Yep. We were there eight weeks, with not many breaks. In fact, we didn't even start painting until the last week! Geez. I was just trying to help.

I worried that our credibility would be jeopardized, along with my leadership. Would I always over-promise what we could do? Was I too pushy? Did I not understand details?

I apologized. We started to shift as a team. We asked tough questions like "What is it that we don't do well? Are we doing random stuff for selfish reasons or because it fits our vision? Where can we add value in the community instead of promoting ourselves?"

Southside Elementary school quickly became our answer. A place we could make a difference. We worked to become a force behind the almost non-existent Parent Teachers Association. We manned the booths at the festivals and open houses. We loved on the teachers. We served on committees and poured money into those efforts. We read with the children. Soon thereafter, with the leadership of the principal and the hard working faculty, Southside became a high progressing school, rising from the fourteenth percentile to the seventy-first percentile! We celebrated.

Our team began to realize what we were good at. Our job was to serve. The question we had from the beginning, "How can we serve you?" was simple and drove us. *We were helpers, not organizers.*

We didn't have lots of money, but through our working partnership with other city groups, we knew of community needs quickly and were able to help provide solutions. We worked against the duplication of services and welcomed all to join us. A same-team approach developed into a ministry partnering system. We invited others to do what they did best, while doing our best to continually serve without pride or pretense, just the goal of sharing God's love.

Homeless? We have a connection for you. Need help with rent? We have a partner that helps you get back on track. Single mother desiring to have a male mentor in your child's life? Check. Children in need of foster families? We had families and resources to quickly connect with partners to provide safe and nurturing environments.

Our next question was, "If we didn't exist, would anyone notice?" We began to take note of the impact God was making on and through us. We celebrated again.

The early failure of a paint job helped our team understand better what we valued. We used our missteps to help establish how we could keep our vision moving forward, not take on too much, and still get much accomplished.

Our mantra was inspired by Winston Churchill's philosophy, "All the great things are simple."

Problem is, going Outside is very complex for most of us, even with early successes. If you're like me, you're afraid of failure. If I'm honest, I can always come up with that one reason we shouldn't go Outside. My fears can lead to struggles with anxiety. Most people wouldn't guess that about me. I usually have a positive attitude, encourage others, succeed, smile, and handle tough situations very well. It would seem I have the ideal personality for being an initiator, instead of being one who struggles with worry.

Occasionally, I'll be sitting in a business meeting or about to speak in public or even when I'm relaxing in the evenings, and it will hit me. A negative thought creeps up. Chest tightens a little. Apprehension sets in. Feelings of stress grip me and I begin to question everything. The heck with going Outside!

Before I ever fully went Outside, my worrisome symptoms had escalated and I needed some answers. "You have a general anxiety disorder," said the doctor. I was relieved it wasn't a major health threat, but still, I was anxious.

Perhaps I had found my forever excuse to stay inside. If an opportunity with uncertainty arose, I could just blame my disorder! As I thought back over my life, I realized that I had always had this type of issue. I wondered what opportunities I missed because of fear and anxiety. I needed a mechanism to cope. Heavy drinking wouldn't work—I tried that route in college. Nothing sounded good. Then I read about Paul's experience:

"So to keep me from becoming conceited because of the surpassing greatness of the revelations, a thorn was given me in the flesh, a messenger of Satan to harass me, to keep me from becoming conceited. Three times I pleaded with the Lord about this, that it should leave me. But he said to me, "My grace is sufficient for you, for my power is made perfect in weakness." Therefore I will boast all the more gladly of my weaknesses, so that the power of Christ may rest upon me. For the sake of Christ, then, I am content with weaknesses, insults, hardships, persecutions, and calamities. For when I am weak, then I am strong" (2 Corinthians 12:7-10).

I wondered, "Is it possible that my weakness could lead to gladness? Is it possible that my anxiety could remind me that successes in my life weren't achieved through my power, but through my weakness?" What if my anxious thoughts were purposed to keep me grounded?

In a weird way, my disorder became a way forward for me. Anxiety was the weakness and, ultimately, the path toward the courage I needed.

True Outsiders don't let their fear stop them. They work to make things better despite the failure they know will come. In 2004, my father was diagnosed with Parkinson's disease. It's tough to watch your father progress in an illness, to lose the ability to drive a car or swing a golf club. Dad acknowledged that he had the disease, but he wasn't going to let it stop his ability to make a difference. So, what did he do?

My father knew that many who have Parkinson's are embarrassed by their condition and they often become hermit like. He also knew that others didn't know how to completely understand what he and some other folks were enduring. So, with a prompting from God, Dad started a local group for people with Parkinson's. As time has passed, Dad isn't able to do as much as he used to. But he does what he can and his attitude reflects it. He refuses to let his thorn break him.

Outsiders recognize their weakness and potential for failure, but don't let it sidetrack them.

*I don't want my life to be explainable
without the Holy Spirit. I want people
to look at my life and know that I
couldn't be doing this by my own power.*
—Francis Chan

Have you ever been to a concert or sports event and sat in the nosebleed section? As you peered through your binoculars to watch what looked like ants running around you couldn't help but notice the people sitting in lower and better seats. But even worse, they were leaving early!

Torrey Smith, a generous and successful business person, grew tired of this, especially for the teams he followed. He wondered, "What if we created a ticket exchange that allows event-goers to either offer their seats, or view the inventory of seats available and then pre-arrange for a ticket exchange right at the event?" Torrey ventured Outside and Jumpseat was born.

As I spoke with Torrey about how he got started he said it was a process of brainstorming, praying, researching, talking with other frustrated fans until he came to the notion that the idea had merit. He met an app developer at a Bible study and hired him to develop the concept. Torrey rolled out the Jumpseat app at the 2013 World Series when he awarded two lucky fans that were sitting in high seats with his lower level seats. He invested more money. Users started to sign up, online exposure increased and Torrey was featured in local media and television. Was this going to be the next huge thing?

Everything seemed to be going forward, but Jumspeat required more time, more resources, more energy. With a growing family and everyday business responsibilities, time passed and the momentum of the launch started to grow weary.

"As an entrepreneur, I love starting new things and being innovative. It's like pursuing a high. It can be addicting. As I think back about the process of starting Jumpseat, I had lots of passion, but I would have done things differently. I became too controlling and didn't involve others for fear they might steal the idea or try to change the concept. I really wanted the app to be successful to the point it could fuel ministry overseas. For that reason and others, I haven't given up on Jumpseat. I've educated myself and believe that God has used this process to grow me."

Most of us can relate to Torrey's story. Maybe you've tried to start something. It didn't go as you planned. It's tainted your desire to try again. But Outsiders like Torrey don't view these experiences as failures, but as tremendous learning experiences.

TAKE ACTION

- Make a list of reasons your vision could fail. What are you doing now to prepare?
- Connect with others going Outside who have experienced failure and quit. What would they have done differently?
- Practice persistence even before you start. It may help to identify your own perseverance hero. Mine is Abraham Lincoln:

    He failed in business in '31, was defeated for state legislature in '32, he tried another business in '33. It failed. His fiancé died in '35. He had a nervous breakdown in '36. In '43, he ran for congress and was defeated. He tried again in '48 and was defeated again. He tried running for the Senate in '55. He lost. The next year he ran for Vice President and lost. In '59, he ran for the Senate again and was defeated. In 1860, the man who signed his name A. Lincoln, was elected the 16th President of the United States.

    The difference between history's boldest accomplishments, and its most staggering failures is often, simply, the diligent will to persevere.[4]

CODE OF SILENCE

Okay. It's time to talk about the Code of Silence. Am I referring to that blockbuster movie in the 1980s where Chuck Norris plays a Chicago cop caught in gang wars? Not hardly, but it is a great excuse to include some facts about Chuck Norris.

You know all of those incredibly awesome Chuck Norris jokes:

Chuck Norris has already been to Mars; that's why there are no signs of life.

Chuck Norris died 20 years ago, death just hasn't built up the courage to tell him yet.

Chuck Norris counted to infinity—twice.[5]

Well, he has a favorite:

They wanted to put Chuck Norris's face on Mount Rushmore, but the granite wasn't hard enough for his beard.

Okay.

The code of silence I am talking about is the condition when a person opts to withhold what is believed to be vital or important information voluntarily or involuntarily. It means zip your lips, lock it with a key, and throw the key away.

I have a mentor who frustrated me with his ability to keep this code. Early on, I found meeting with him pointless. Other than the occasional clarifying questions, he sat there unmoved. I would cringe when thinking about our time together but for some reason I kept crawling back to meet again and again. He was comfortable with long pauses. I, however, would continue rambling and speaking in circles ending nowhere. What was so luring about these times together?

At first I thought maybe he couldn't hear me. Especially since we usually met in buzzing coffee shops or busy restaurants. I'd talk a few minutes and as I hesitated, he knew I still wasn't done, so he sat there and smiled graciously. I nervously laughed it off and kept going. I'd often have that moment at lunch with him when I noticed his food was gone and that my entire meal was untouched. (That embarrassing moment you realize you've done every bit of the talking.) To be honest, I was much younger then this mentor and intimidated by his experience, confidence, and deep relationship with God. I felt like a gnat flying around the room that needed to be swatted.

I just wanted him to tell me what to do, but all he did was listen. Why listen! He had the critical information I needed. I wanted to open his head and grab it out, but that was a probably a bad idea too. At some point, I woke up from my school boy daze and started to understand what he was doing. He knew I was a bad listener and that the best advice for me was to show me how to not give advice, but to listen. I feel like such an idiot now. Man, I was so self-centered. That was the beginning of my efforts to learn the code and how to listen well.

Our closing time together usually consisted of a few questions with open-ended answers. It was only when I left our meeting that clarity would arrive. His gracious way of listening prompted me to wonder how much further I could go if I learned to listen, especially to what God has to say? Oooooooohhhhhhhh.

Even though Outsiders are great learners, we tend to be poor listeners. We want to forge ahead and not slow down—who's got time for that? But, how many times have we risked offending someone with our lack of listening? Consider this listening checklist and see how well you are doing:

☐ First, put down your phone, computer, tablet, and (insert name of distracting device here). Resist the urge to peek at said device mid-conversation.

☐ Pay attention to non-verbals. Control yours by making eye contact. Watch theirs as well and adjust your conversation accordingly.

☐ Don't interrupt. Even if you think you have something important to say. Let them finish.

☐ Make an effort to understand their opinions and feelings. Don't spend the time they are talking formulating your own thoughts.

☐ Take notes if it helps you focus and retain information, but only if it's not distracting.

☐ Ask follow-up questions to clarify your understanding.

☐ Give them time to formulate their answers without offering a response or solution.

See what I mean? Are you listening?

I'm continually amazed by Jesus and his willingness to be a good listener.

Immediately after his resurrection in Luke 24, we find Jesus walking alongside Cleopas and a friend as they discussed everything that happened to him on the cross. He didn't interject or even make his identity known. He simply asked helpful questions and listened to their answers. Even after he rose from the dead, he was a good listener.

"He knew all people and needed no one to bear witness about man, for He himself knew what was in man." (John 2:24).

Here's the crazy part. *If Jesus is aware of what is in our hearts before we even say it, why does he need to listen?* Perhaps the answer is found in compassion. Could you imagine sitting with Jesus, him looking directly into your eyes and listening to your every word? Oh my. That's powerful stuff. After considering the ministry of Jesus and his perfect listening skills, I had to get better. I wanted to develop a code of silence. What if the famous quote by St. Francis of Assisi, "Preach the Gospel at all times and when necessary use words," wasn't just about sharing God's love by letting your actions speak? What if it was about developing the ability to be silent—a code of silence? Outsiders can make a real difference with our listening. Wouldn't this encourage our friends to listen to the source they need and not our often-biased opinions?

Randy Bates is my good friend and it's not just because we are both avid Kentucky basketball fans. When I met him he was living in a downtown retirement/assisted living facility. In the morning, Randy would start his day be heading out to visit people on Main Street. He had his normal stops. Wherever Randy went, he knew everyone and everyone knew him. He'd ask about people's children and he could always recall their birthdays.

It's hard not to notice Randy's steady demeanor. His kindness and thoughtfulness towards others. Randy doesn't have a ton of personal possessions, but he really doesn't want for much; he just wants to be your friend. I learned what a great listener he was. Each time we come back together, he asks about our last conversation and the current circumstances in my life. Randy is a great listener and Randy always has time for me.

As an Outsider, we must learn how to listen to God. I think about Mary sitting at the feet of Jesus "listening to what He said," (Luke 10:39) so focused in on His words that she didn't care about the work needing to be done. Jesus said Mary was "choosing what was better." As Outsiders, we must learn to do the same.

TAKE ACTION

- Go through the listening checklist one more time. Practice using the tips in your next conversation.
- Ask a close friend to be honest with you about your listening skills. Don't defend yourself, just listen.
- Practice listening while praying to God. Ask questions, then be quiet.

---

*"Let us be silent, that we may hear
the whisper of God."
Ralph Waldo Emerson*

BE READY FOR CURVEBALLS

Senator Harry Truman never expected to be nominated vice president. He and most everyone knew that when President Franklin D. Roosevelt would be elected for the fourth time, he wouldn't make it through his final term. To make it even more disconcerting, whoever would be elected vice president would presumably become president during a time of war. Harry was a humble man with integrity. He was floored when he was selected as second in command.

To make matters more challenging, Truman was seldom contacted or consulted by his commander-in-chief once he was in office. President Roosevelt only met with Truman alone two times. Imagine Truman's shock when Eleanor Roosevelt informed him that her husband had died eighty-two days into his vice presidential term. When he extended his condolences to Mrs. Roosevelt, she famously retorted "Is there anything we can do for you? You are the one in trouble now!"

Shortly after taking the oath of office, Truman was known to have said to reporters, "Boys, if you ever pray, pray for me now. I don't know if you fellows ever had a load of hay fall on you, but when they told me what happened yesterday, I felt like the moon, the stars and all the planets had fallen on me."[6]

For Outsiders, many of us never thought we'd be up on

deck in the big game of life. As it was for Truman, the great unknown is a little scary, like being a batter, standing nervous at the plate, not sure what pitch to expect next. The only sure thing is the thing we fight against—curve balls. Once we think we have it licked, here comes the off-speed pitch.

Coach Jim "Hos" Wiley has coached American Legion baseball for 35 years. Recently inducted to the state hall of fame, he's also served as a scout to the New York Yankees. Suffice to say, he's seen plenty of baseball over the years and remains very passionate about the sport.

In a conversation I had with Coach Wiley he said, "In life, what stops us from doing something big for God is when someone throws us a curve ball. We don't expect it and ultimately lose contact with all we're doing. Rarely do we spend time getting ready for the unexpected. Baseball is like the game of life and in order to hit the

> *When life throws you a curve ball, it's the lifetime of an opportunity to knock it out of the park.*
> *– Unknown*

curve ball, your first need is to concentrate. This starts before you even get in the batter's box. Good hitters watch pitchers from the dugout. They look for a pitcher's tendencies because they know a pitcher will have watched their hitting tendencies too. Good hitters will pick up the pitch early and follow it all the way to home plate. They don't assume anything. Coaches often tell batters, don't swing at the curve, and just hit the fast ball when it comes."

Coach Wiley doesn't subscribe to that theory.

He says, "Players have to be able to hit the curve ball. Not being able to connect on a curve ball is what keeps them from going to the big leagues. It's important to think fastball, but always be ready for the curve."

Often Coach Wiley will tell his players, "Be aggressive. Don't get behind in the count. Swing at the first pitch, you might catch the pitcher off guard. Don't worry if you're not perfect when you strike out, but know which type of pitch struck you out. Be prepared the next time. Go to the cage and practice after the game on the pitch you struggle with."

In being assertive, Coach Wiley believes in getting ahead early. He advises, "The longer an 'at bat' goes on and the game goes on, the less likely the batter will be able to surprise the pitcher. Then, the other team puts in the relief pitcher and he shuts you down. Then you're done."

Like Coach Wiley, I love to work in youth sports. On a much smaller level, I've coached various sports in recreation leagues for over fifteen years. When we work with the kids, we say, "Get up on your toes!" They always think it's so funny. No, I'm not trying to get them to do a rock star toe-stand; I'm trying to get them off their heels. If you keep all your weight on the back of your feet, you lose your agility and balance very easily. Try it. If the ball or someone comes directly at you, you're liable to end up on your back looking at your toes—that's not what we want!

It doesn't feel good to stay on your toes all the time. It's certainly not comfortable. But, in order to advance your mission Outside, you must learn to stay "ready" and expect the unexpected. Don't get caught up trying to prevent the unforeseen from happening, because it's coming. Outsiders learn that the unexpected will help you strengthen your vision and will help make the vision become a reality.

I quit baseball early in life. I was done. Guess why? I was afraid of the ball—especially the one that would curve into my lower back. I didn't want to put in the work. I just wanted to hit the straight pitch. I was never focused. God promises that he won't leave you, but he doesn't promise us all the details. *The curves in the journey only shape us for better doing his will.* Outsiders learn to expect the curve and don't get dismayed when it comes.

TAKE ACTION

- What have you noticed about the preparedness of successful Outsiders?
- Start making contact today by developing your written game plan. Take into account the curve balls that might come your way.
- Are you confident yet, or do you need the guidance of a coach? Identify and approach a potential mentor within the next five days.

Element Four: Logistics

"...For here we have no lasting city, but we seek the city that is to come..."

DON'T QUIT YOUR DAY JOB (UNLESS YOU NEED TO)

Jon Walker is one of those friends that you get to know in a small town—the kind of friend that after years and years of living in central Kentucky, you begin to form deep relationships after going to school together, playing sports together, and getting into mischief together. In later years, I'd catch up with Jon coming and going, but I couldn't have guessed what would happen when he called me out of the blue one day. He said, "Hey Webb, we're looking for property for our business—can you help?" While the initial process would be business oriented, I had a peculiar feeling. Like many times in the marketplace, I knew this wasn't just about real estate.

We started looking for property, catching up on old memories, laughing about playing soccer together—it kick-started our friendship all over again. One Sunday Jon brought his family to our church. This seemed easy enough; it happened to be just down the street from his mother's house. Jon and his family felt at ease and enjoyed the welcoming approach we were working to develop.

Jon stood in the back when he first came to church. As each gathering passed, he became more interested and began to sit and listen. Until one week he was jarred beyond words. He came to me and said, "I think I'm ready."

"Ready for what?" I replied, thinking he was still talking about the real estate search.

"I'm ready to give my life to Jesus and be baptized," he said. My mouth dropped and my heart leapt.

What happened in Jon's story is a true testimony of how the workplace can intertwine with sharing faith. In Acts, we read that one of the greatest missionary-initiators, the Apostle Paul, "worked as a tentmaker" and "he reasoned in the synagogue with both Jews and God-fearing Greeks, as well as in the marketplace day by day with those who happened to be there." (Acts 18:13 & 18) God set apart Paul for this specific purpose and ministry and it helped my thinking tremendously. I began to wonder why more Christ followers weren't following Paul's example as God had inspired him to write to the church in Corinth:

"Even though I am free of the demands and expectations of everyone, I have voluntarily become a servant to any and all in order to reach a wide range of people: religious, nonreligious, meticulous moralists, loose-living immoralists, the defeated, the demoralized—whoever. I didn't take on their way of life. I kept my bearings in Christ—but I entered their world and tried to experience things from their point of view. I've become just about every sort of servant there is in my attempts to lead those I meet into a God-saved life. I did all this because of the Message. I didn't just want to talk about it; I wanted to be in on it (1 Corinthians 9:21-23 MSG).

My friend Matt, a fellow believer in the real estate business recently admitted, "Before, I was selling real estate and following Jesus on the side. Now, I've learned to follow Jesus first and sell real estate on the side."

I've always had multiple community involvements including ministry. If I left my real estate career, it would have hurt my ability to keep going in the work God was doing. I learned that my calling was inside of my job not on the sidelines while I was at work. Keeping my job, helped me sustain relationships *Outside* the walls of the church or in the unexpected circles of ministry. It helped me leverage local influence—just to be a "regular" guy put me in real situations. Sure it's messy, but it gave me a gateway to meet and reconnect with people like Jon. For me, these stories happened often and were huge affirmations, even though others found my daily activity puzzling or unsustainable.

Undoubtedly, often times it was hard to keep my head straight. To some, I was a real estate guy—to others, I was a crazy Outsider who loved Jesus. It wasn't a well formed strategy on my part. *Perhaps my calling was unique, but I didn't feel my roles were mutually exclusive.* Ultimately, I could see God working through it all.

Perhaps I had every reason to leave my job. Perhaps I needed to choose between going Outside and my nine to five, but to my amazement, my continuing to work in real estate seemed to be working, and lives within the community were changed based on who I was able to connect people with.

"And my God will supply every need of yours according to his riches in glory in Christ Jesus."
Philippians 4:19 (NIV)

Back to Jon's story. With this altering change in his life and due to health circumstances, Jon began to also think about his business. He wondered, "Is this what I need to spend most of my time doing?' Do I need to keep my company and job or leave?"

Jon was developing his faith, growing in mercy towards others and reading the scriptures. The practice of following Jesus by going Outside became a genuine desire for him. He and his wife decided it was time for him to leave his company. He didn't know what he'd be doing for income, but he left because it became evident it was the right time and thing to do.

To Jon's great surprise, he was later approached by a nonprofit ministry focused on sharing the love of God with others. Through his new job, he could impact lives on a daily basis by sharing his business savvy and past struggles.

If you asked Jon today, he'd tell you he never would have seen himself taking such a great leap of faith or working such a job. Jon took a risk and left the business world to fulfill his calling Outside.

The job decision is a complicated one for many. It could be the biggest hurdle you currently have. Many people struggle with it. You're not alone. It takes time to determine. If you aren't sure, keep going where you are. God doesn't want you to be confused and He will make it clear in time. Going Outside almost always requires risk financially. Begin to prepare yourself today for what you think is going to be most effective. Too many times, people with a sincere motive to go Outside are encumbered by prior financial decisions and current burdens—money stops the vision before it even starts.

Jess Correll, a community bank owner, knows that borrowing money can be dangerous—strong words, especially for a banker. Gaining the wisdom of being debt free, his organization retired its debt in 1994 and resolved to remain a low debt company. By doing so, Jess began to arrange his organization as an entity with no chains—ready to capitalize on opportunity. It has also freed his team to be extremely generous with their profits and help many in need. Jess will tell you that his dreams were made possible by intentional choices made long ago.

This financial lesson of preparedness can apply to all Outsiders. As, Outsiders we must get and keep our financial house in order. It's not easy. It requires sacrifice—you might not get everything you want. But, when God calls you to move, leave your job, take a step of faith, or do something generally crazy—money won't stand in the way. You'll be ready to go Outside.

TAKE ACTION

- Consider how your current job plays a role in your vision. Will it make you more or less effective in going

Outside?

- If you have decided you'll need to leave your current job now or later, consider the obstacles. What are some ways to overcome those potential hindrances?
- If God has led you to keep your job, make a list of ways you can "lean in" and go Outside by staying where you are.
- Take a close look at your financial state of affairs. Make a list of current income and expenses. Now make a list of future income and expenses based on your vision. List both small and big choices you can implement today that will help you get past difficulties later.
- Count the cost of *not* being prepared to go Outside— not just financially, but emotionally, physically, relationally and spiritually.

FIND A
PAINT STORE

My new headquarters for "operation go Outside" was a paint store. Random, I know, but it was free (props to the owner, my friend BJ) and it was the perfect place to chase our vision—directly in the heart of our city, off the sidewalks of Main Street. The tall windows of the store illuminated the colorful space where a group of us would meet and challenge each other to step outside of our comfort zones and dream a little. Something about a huge wall of paint chips made that a little easier.

Want to hear something curious about that store? We were there to brainstorm ways to serve people in our community. Fatefully, we were often interrupted by the *people in our community* barging in the paint store in the middle of our conversations. They smelled the coffee. The light was on. Lovely, right? Well, confession time. My blood pressure would rise and my mind would churn, "What an inconvenience," "How rude," or "We'll never get done in time!" There were even times when I considered moving our meetings to somewhere more private so we could protect our limited time together. Boy am I glad the intruders kept coming. Those stoppages shook us out of our neatly-controlled simmer and reminded us of why were there in the first place—to connect with people.

Christ Jesus, who, though he was in the form of God, did not count equality with God a thing to be grasped, but emptied himself, by taking the form of a

Now to him who is able to do far more abundantly than all we ask or think, according to his power at work within us.
Ephesians 3:20

servant, being born in the likeness of men (Philippians 2:5-7).

Sometimes, the place you meet—your paint store—can either stifle or promote your vision. That is why the pressure to choose the right location can be overwhelming. In my work as a commercial real estate broker for almost twenty years, I have seen countless businesses go belly-up due to hang-ups over their location.

Maybe your place is a building. It might be a local café or even the park. But maybe it's not a physical place at all. According to the Pew Research Center, 74% of online adults use social networking sites.[7] NewsCred found that 329 million people read blogs every month. And those numbers continue to grow.[8] Normal people like you and like me are finding that the Internet is often the easiest and most effective place to pursue their vision.

In 2009, Megan Terry started a blog. Her family was adopting from the Democratic Republic of the Congo and she wanted to be able to update family and friends on their progress. For the first few months, her readers were people she knew in real life. Her mom, her neighbor, her friend from college. But things changed, as Megan explains:

About six months into blogging, folks started sharing our blog with others and all of a sudden there were strangers reading. For a while, I felt like I had to make my "corner of the internet" pleasing for people. I wrote what I thought other people wanted to read. It felt fake and superficial.

Our son had a rough transition coming into our family. I felt like a failure because I thought that I should be better at being an adoptive mother. After all, so many people had prayed for our son and helped us along on our adoption journey. Finally, the point came when I let loose and started writing from a very honest voice of just how hard adoption was—for us and for our son. I wrote about how there were days I felt like I was just our son's babysitter and how I just felt like I couldn't keep all the balls in the air. I wrote about my struggle with depression after adoption. I put it all out there—warts and all. That's when things on my blog took off.

When Megan started writing about the messy parts of her life and her family's adoption experiences, *Millions of Miles* gained millions of readers. It blew up.

The best part of finding my "tribe" on the Internet is that it gives me a platform to advocate for the things I am passionate about—moms and vulnerable kids. My readers helped me raise tens of thousands of dollars to help keep families in impoverished nations together. They also invested in maternal health and education for girls and women at risk in developing nations. By building a following, I was able to give my audience an opportunity to help people on the other side of the world.

Still stressed about space?

Here are two important things to remember about your location.

1. **It doesn't have to be perfect.** In fact, it may not be a physical location at all. If you stay true to your vision and the "who" and "why" questions, the "where" answers will follow.

2. **It's probably not permanent anyway**. Our group met in the paint store for a year. Our plans for serving our community mandated more space –space we didn't have and certainly couldn't afford to buy. Yet somehow, in the nick of time, we were given the opportunity to

use our local elementary school for free. And we have moved again since then to an even larger location, where (you guessed it) we pay *zero* rent.

As you sift through the logistics of where your vision will unfold, remember that the outcome of your journey will not be bound by your location. Be flexible and be prepared for God to provide just exact place that you need to go Outside.

TAKE ACTION

- Reflect on the places and people that you are most drawn to. Record what you appreciate about each of them.
- Think creatively and invite people to help you like BJ helped me.
- Be ready to hear "No" and for things to not work out. Don't get hung up on the cost of a building, fixed time tables or even finding the perfect domain name.
- You might be overwhelmed at this point. Make a list and keep working it item by item. Keep searching, and keep the conversation going.

"Courage is not simply one of the virtues, but the form of every virtue at the testing point."
– C. S. Lewis

AT A CROSSROADS

Brook Brotzman. If I heard that name ten times, I heard it a hundred. My list of friends that were being impacted personally by him and taking trips to the Dominican Republic seemed to grow daily. Brook's involvement and worldwide efforts to share the love of Jesus with the disadvantaged sounded very inspiring. Finally one morning over breakfast, my friend introduced me. After just a few minutes, I could tell Brook was an Outsider.

Brook and I ended up having coffee together. I was impressed with his high energy level and willingness to cut through the unnecessary tape to make things happen. Not to wait on permission to help people. One night I called Brook and he was on his way home from visiting some former students who had been impacted by his ministry. I took the chance to ask him more deeply about his story.

Being a former youth minister from rural Illinois, Brook had a passion for teaching his students about God's love and compassion. Psalm 34:18 tells us, "The Lord is close to the brokenhearted and saves those who are crushed in spirit."

He was compelled to show his students the heart of God through a first-hand experience with people who were poor and hurting.

Trips to the inner-city of Chicago and Philadelphia shifted

his thoughts further abroad. If people in our first-world country were hurting, surely those in impoverished countries were even more so.

Brook could have stopped there. But he didn't. Brook would eventually establish GO Ministries, which allowed him to partner with over 100 indigenous Christian pastors and leaders, feeding over 1,000 children a hot meal six days a week through one of nine nutrition centers, offering education to over 600 children through its primary school, partnering with over 30 churches in the Dominican and Haiti, facilitating twelve sports leagues with at risk youth, and offering medical aid to the poor through a daily medical clinic.[10]

Brook tells starters, "Do all the research you can, but it won't take shape until you step out in faith. It's only then that God will put the road in front of you. The Bridge won't be built until you put your foot into the creek." As Indiana Jones found out, only the man of faith shall pass. Most of us spend our lives bound up in fear, but what's the worst thing that can happen to you? You fail? If so, you've probably done ten times more than ten others around you. God will validate the faith you show. Like Brook said, "You just have to GO." But, how do we just GO? Often times, we find ourselves standing right at the crossroads. The junction where Outside and inside meet. Tell me, which one you would take:

> *"As each has received a gift, use it to serve one another, as good stewards of God's varied grace."*
> *1 Peter 4:10*

Option 1) Interstate Inside. Easy transition, smooth and relaxing, plenty of time, amenities for good travel are always accessible, views of mountains without having to cross them, elk and antelope run beside you and smile, heavy traffic is backed up on the other side of the median – not on yours, and the outcome is pretty controlled. The destination will be easily achieved and there is plenty of money for gas. Success and happiness is just ahead.

Option 2) Highway Outside. Likely to have issues getting started, a rocky ride full of curves and hills, debris, construction, cross winds, minivans and semi-trucks everywhere, no potty breaks for miles, worn out surfaces, uninsured drivers, toll roads that don't take credit cards, and bottleneck delays are unavoidable. High level of faith is required. Patience is not optional. Control is entrusted to someone else. Joy is available—so long as you don't allow it to be stolen.

"Stand at the crossroads and look; ask for the ancient paths, ask where the good way is, and walk in it, and you will nd rest for your souls. But you said, 'We will not walk in it.'"
— Jeremiah 6:16 (NIV)

As you can see, Interstate Inside is pretty appealing. It's the one most travelled. Yet, chances are God is calling you take the Outsider path. Once you said yes to Jesus, God gave you at least one spiritual gift and that gift wasn't for you to hoard. It was given to you as an Outsider to administer the grace God has shown you—to be a good steward. No doubt, someone else needs to hear about that same love. You probably won't find that person traveling along on your comfy Interstate Insider path. Sharing your gifts, talents, and resources while displaying the grace only He can give isn't happening if all you ever do is stay put.

For Outsider like Brook, the inside route wasn't even an option. Brook wouldn't let normal reasons and complacency keep him from going. He said, "I wanted my life to count for more than just being successful. I looked at how Jesus measured things. I realized that I needed to take one little step. I knew I couldn't do it all, but I said to myself, 'I'm just going to do this one thing for somebody else.' I found the joy and comfort that God brings. He will give you courage to take the next step, then the next step, then the next. With proper perspective you become empowered as opposed to overwhelmed."

When things were just getting started, Brook borrowed $10,000 from a home equity loan to buy a van for ministry use. "It felt like a million bucks," Brook recalled. While visiting a particular fam-

> *I prayed for twenty years but received no answer until I prayed with my legs.*
> *- Frederick Douglass*

ily about his vision and needs, they handed him an envelope. He left that night and gave it to one of his students to open. It was a check for exactly $10,000! Brook said, "That taught me a valuable lesson about living by faith. Our ministry projects started at $500. Then they went to $5,000, then to $50,000. We got to $500,000, which turned into $5 million and now it's $25 million dollar projects. But it all started with that $10,000 blessing and the lesson we learned." Brook's vision surged beyond what he ever thought was possible.

The difference between being an Outsider or something else is simple. Outsiders start right where they are. They focus on one day, one step, one person, one conversation, and one need. They don't mind strategy sessions, but don't get jammed up by them either. It's likely that many, many, everyday people have the great potential to be real Outsider—to be on the front row of seeing the world changed. It all starts at the crossroads and that one step—it's a huge one. But in their heart, God has shown them that passion without action is pointless.

Just get started and you'll find your beginning.

TAKE ACTION

- Based on your current actions, would you consider yourself to be cruising along on Interstate Inside or navigating Highway Outside?
- Read the book of Esther in the Bible. Focus on Chap-

ters 3-9. What small but significant steps did Esther take to fulfill the calling and position God had placed her in? Consider your journey in light of the account of Esther.

- Prayerfully, today, there is one simple thing you could do to get started. It might seem trivial, but it's a step. What is it? What if you stopped where you are and took that step right now?

- Once you take the first step, it might lead to a few more action points. What are they? Write them down and ask someone to make sure you get them started as well.

BEWARE OF INSIDERS

I was eating and chatting with a large table of folks at a chamber of commerce gathering. We were discussing the challenges in our community—non-profits struggling to meet the necessities, the future generation's lack of interest in faith, a growing heroine epidemic, split-homes and parents not getting involved with their kids at school, a growing lack of unity. I causally said under my breath and a mouth full of mashed potatoes, "Well, you know if the local church would engage with the community instead of waiting for the community to come to them, there wouldn't be much of a problem."

A flame was sparked.

The table got quiet.

My face turned red. I cleared my throat and stared at the food on my plate. My plans were known. My idea of what it meant to go Outside—my particular story of going Outside—had officially escaped the confines of my brain. Finally. Still looking down, I squeezed my eyes shut. Maybe the program had started and their attention had turned to the main stage. Yes, that would explain the silence. I raised my head to find the entire table of twelve looking directly at me. The barrage of verbals and non-verbals that came next almost sent me off my chair.

It appeared that half the table wanted to leap up and give me a huge high five. "Where is this new thing happening? How can I help? Have you started? What's your website?" Of course, I had scarce details and no website—just the Outside vision. But it was exciting to see people catch fire. Maybe I wasn't crazy. I swallowed my potatoes and took a drink of sweet tea and almost swallowed my lemon when I noticed the other half of the table looked like they had just eaten a lemon too.

> *Nobody goes where the crowds are anymore. It's too crowded.*
> *— Yogi Berra*

The people around the table were speaking paragraphs without saying anything at all. For them, immediate heartburn was setting in. Tum *tum* tum tum tum. It made me want to reach for some antacids too. Their thoughts were predictable. *We don't need that. That won't work. It's just fluff.*

To go Outside is to understand that not everyone will share your passion. Some will still be encouraging and speak well of you and your calling, even when they don't understand. Others have developed a mentality against anything Outside. These people won't *go*. They are content to stay inside, thank you very much. Some might even get combative with you. Especially if your vision puts their comfort at risk. I can actually handle those people better than their passive aggressive cohorts.

"Oh my, how much money will it cost to do that?"

"I love your passion. You're welcome back whenever you find what it is you're looking for."

"I'm getting tired just thinking about what you just said."

"Why did you have to leave to start this?"

"Hmmmmm. Interesting."

"Bless their hearts." (A Southern favorite.)

Here's a glance at a short list of Insider hallmarks that can help you identify what you're up against:

- Insiders talk lots about the "way we do it," or the "way

we've always done it."

- Insiders invite you in, but for their purposes, not to advance a new cause.
- Insiders want to keep Outsiders close. Think middle school bully.
- Insiders are interested in guarding their job, protecting their title and maintaining control.
- Insiders sometimes have pure motives but are fearful of what might happen if things get uncomfortable.
- Insiders love receiving credit and the spotlight. Rarely will they promote someone else's Outside thinking.
- Insiders don't like it when Outsiders do something crazy. When they complain, you're probably on the right path.
- Your vision will melt if you wait for the approval of an Insider.
- Insiders are everywhere. Sometimes even your closest friends can be disguised as Insiders.
- Insiders know how to kill new ideas by using crafty methods of slow play and avoidance.
- Insiders are glad to let you run ahead and conveniently pull their support when things get hot in the kitchen.

The truth is that we have all struggled with playing the role of an Insider at some point. It's the easy route. As Outsiders, we must show grace and not become bitter or distracted. With persistence, a true movement from God can't be stopped even when others try to dismantle it.

So how do we remain persistent? We don't let the fear of what others will say (or not say) discourage us from sharing our ideas. Even when we feel vulnerable, we keep sharing. Even when we feel lonely as we sort out our unique vision, we keep sharing. Even when we don't have answers for all of the critics, we keep sharing.

When my wife was the student speaker at her college graduation, she shared one of her favorite quotes. It is called the Man in the Arena, delivered in 1910 by Theodore Roosevelt.

It is not the critic who counts; not the man who points out how the strong man stumbles, or where the doer of deeds could have done them better. The credit belongs to the man who is actually in the arena, whose face is marred by dust and sweat and blood; who strives valiantly; who errs, who comes short again and again, because there is no effort without error and shortcoming; but who does actually strive to do the deeds; who knows great enthusiasms, the great devotions; who spends himself in a worthy cause; who at the best knows in the end the triumph of high achievement, and who at the worst, if he fails, at least fails while daring greatly, so that his place shall never be with those cold and timid souls who neither know victory nor defeat.

Get out in the arena and never look back.

TAKE ACTION

- Affirmation often comes much later then when an Outsider first steps out. For me, I can recall getting a note several years subsequent to my Going Outside from my friend Tony: "God has done a great thing in our community because you accepted a vision from the Master and sought to embody it and pursue it. Well done, good and faithful servant." If I had waited for that in the beginning, would I have ever heard those words? Are you willing to wait for affirmation that will come later?
- People will ask you questions that you might not be able to answer. The unknown may cause others to be uncomfortable and may raise doubts within yourself. Don't let their unwillingness or negativity interrupt your journey. Be honest. Get good at saying, "I don't know the answer to your question yet, but here's what I do know so far."

- Respect others' opinions, even if they don't align with yours. Don't debate. Encourage and move on.
- How will you be empathize with the Insider viewpoint, but not allow yourself to be hindered?

Element Five: Beyond

"...Through him then let us continually offer up a sacrifice of praise to God, that is, the fruit of lips that acknowledge his name..."

BAD IDEA

Starting a church is a really bad idea.

Well, unless it's a calling from God.

Unless God calls you in the middle of the night when you can't sleep and then plants this one idea in your brain that just won't go away. Then, it promises to be a rewarding, thrilling, rejuvenating, strenuous, and roller coaster of a ride. For our family, it was wonderful.

Our church started in a Main Street retail store through the generosity of a paint store owner (yep *that* paint store) who gave us his key to use on Sunday afternoons. It grew. We moved to a home—my home to be exact. As momentum continued to build, we needed a public place to welcome people. We found an elementary school with a principal who took a gamble on us. Susie Burkhardt had every reason to say no, and who would have blamed her? Susie, however, said yes and allowed us to use the building and classrooms each weekend. God kept growing the mission. We loved the school and didn't want to leave, but it was being demolished and rebuilt. Without a place to gather, would our dream end here?

With little options, a businessman stepped in to buy a large retail center under distress. He said, "Lee, if you partner with me to lease and manage the space outside of the church unit, we'll do it. Plus, no rent for the church." Wow. 13,000 square feet with no rent! The church grew. We needed more kids' space. No problem. This same businessman would offer the church more space to expand. Still no rent. The movement was nonstop as the vision continued to be pursued.

"Don't bother to give God instructions; just report for duty."
– Corrie ten Boom

As Outsiders, our people desired an outpost to serve another section of the city we loved. A vacant building that belonged to a local restaurant owner kept coming to mind. We asked and he graciously stepped in. "Sure, you can use the building no problem. Just tell me what you need me to do to the space. Oh by the way, no rent."

Many times along the way we questioned the finances—who wouldn't? We would drive by a location and would say, "We don't have the money, but, man . . . that spot would be awesome!" Heck, even after we knew we wouldn't have to pay rent, we'd still come up with reasons why it wouldn't work. When our church family didn't have the resources to build out the retail center space and improve for church use, we'd pray and keep sharing the story. Amazing things kept happening. Our small congregation would raise an offering in one day for $78,483.89. We'd raise another $50,000 after we got in the space for more needs. This is an organization that ran on a $100,000 annual budget just a year before. Take that, you pesky finances!

We believed God was saying to us, "Keep Going and you'll see just how much I'm for you!" As we did our best to love God and love people, we were able to build influence and trust. Our team had a shared and deep desire to be a part of something bigger then ourselves.

It was about everyone playing their role and not trying to be a player.

In the end, we believed that's why people helped us. We

stayed true to who we were. We had a calling and clear vision. We didn't want to be held captive beyond our dreams to serve and give generously. We invited others into the work God was and is doing.

People were excited about the possibility of our big ideas and that we had the courage to even dream such a dream. We learned about generosity and the stewardship responsibility it brings. We learned that if you have a clear and simple vision, trust in God's will and have faith in Jesus—money is not an issue.

By now, you've probably put it together that the very vision that lead me to leave a church led me to start one. You've also probably realized I never quit my day job to be a church planter. I enjoyed being with business people and other starters trying to conquer the world. I can honestly say I don't know how those five years worked out. Church planting, especially as a volunteer leader, takes lots of dedication and hard work. And time. So does owning your own business. *So does trying to do both at the same time.*

How did that work out financially? How did we have the persistence to keep going? God provided and we followed, and although the exciting adventure to "go Outside" started with a church plant for our family, it didn't end there. It would continue to show up in our everyday lives.

What have I done?

As I peeked around the corner holding our one year old on my side, panic set in. We were out on limb now. There was absolutely no going back. The kitchen renovation had started and boy had it started. The floor was full of insulation, which meant the ceiling was no

> *"Great indeed are our opportunities, great also is our responsibility."*
> *– William Wilberforce*

longer in place—so I gradually raised my head and saw the bare rafters. This was seriously scary. My eyes began to bulge as I thought about the scene in *The Money Pit* where the bathtub drops through the ceiling and crashes onto the floor below.[10] Why did we do this? Trying not to let the anxiety lead to full on panic, I took a deep breath and said, "Oh noooooo. What have I done?"

That's what it feels like to go Outside. *Where's the real life UNO reverse card? Can I get a retraction here?* Seeking the best ways to cope, I usually start long conversations in my head that can go on for an entire day. *How can I get back to where I was before this whole thing got kicked off, before I told those people what I was doing? I just want to be a normal person again.*

These moments

> "You may do your duty without love; but you cannot love without doing your duty."
> — Ravi Zacharias

of actuality bring up questions I often feel bad for even asking, "When will this be over? *When do I get to leave?*"

Like many other Outsiders, by nature, I'm a starter, not a manager. I run with a line of entrepreneurs and enjoy talking with them about all the things they started. I'll ask questions and wait for answers. Over the years, one of my favorites to ask, "How long does it take to turn the corner—to become successful for most businesses?" The most common reply has been five years. The first year is investigation, and you spend countless hours and money trying to get going. Then the following two years, it's nothing but hard work. Perhaps by the fourth or fifth year you've seen some real progress." *Five years!* This is absurd. For many of us, instant gratification never comes fast enough.

As excited as you are in the beginning, Outsiders learn they are in for many ups and downs. Each day brings victory and challenge. Often, the challenge makes you want to flee your responsibility, but as the vision moves forward, your ownership deepens, and your commitment grows stronger, you know you have to stick it out. It might not take five years; it might take many more or even less. God can even call an Outsider to a certain path for a lifetime.

One Sunday I was about to baptize a young mother who had previously known nothing of church life. I thought to myself, *I can't believe this is happening.* Which was the longer shot? That she would take this faith step or that I would be in such a position? I also remember great affirmation seeing a new church attendee bum cigarettes in the back of the worship area—instead of throwing him out, we made sure he felt completely comfortable and welcome. So many moments gave such great satisfaction, like the Sunday my grandmother, in her nineties, came to church and sat by an African American friend of mine who was in her eighties. How incredible was this, to witness God bridging history and gaps between people who would have never worshipped together on earth before?

Experiences like these made everything worthwhile.

I was reminded of Jesus and the moments after he was baptized. The Spirit of God came to rest on Him, and then a voice from Heaven said, "This is my beloved son, with whom I am well pleased." I would just contemplate on the son of God and his relationship with his heavenly father. I tried to imagine how extraordinarily

> "Never quit something with great long-term potential just because you can't deal with the stress of the moment."
> – Seth Godin

powerful that moment was. My desire grew to please my heavenly father and to do his will for my life. Who cares how long this takes and what people think! It was as if God was saying to me, "Great job, son . . . I'm so proud of you!"

I was done asking, "When can I leave?" I began asking "How long can I stay?"

When it comes to this point, Outsiders often experience a great release and realization that leads to a further sense of calling and duty. I said to myself, *this is it.* Here's what I learned:

Knowing when to leave can only be realized *after*

you've fully surrendered yourself to the vision God has given you.

Too often, I work with small business owners and starters who quit too early. They don't understand duty. The rainbows and cotton candy feelings fade away and nothing is left but the mundane.

Outsiders have to push through. Stop looking for someone else to do the job that has been placed in front of you. When things get hard, don't become a Debbie Downer. Do what it takes. Scrub toilets, pick up trash, encourage others, take risks, have the hard conversations, spend less, save more, go slow, stick with it.

Honestly, it can be really, really hard.

Especially as it relates to living out a faith journey "outside the gates." In my own personal experience, obstacles fueled my perseverance, but it would have been easy to let them block it and lose faith in my calling. God surrounded Rachel and I with lots of great friends to hold us up and teach us about daily persistence. One such family had a daughter, Kendra that loved to help us with our kiddos. She would afford us the opportunity for an occasional date night and along the way, she shared her story and faith journey with us. Here's Kendra's story:

> *I have to start off by saying that things are not always what they seem and neither are people. Growing up in a Christian home as a missionary kid, you'd think everything was perfect.*
>
> *However, there were some questions spiraling in my head. Questions about God. "What if everything I've been taught isn't true? What if there isn't a God? What if life did happen by chance? And even if there was a God, would he really love me anyway?"*
>
> *The questions choked me and I kept them inside; I couldn't tell anybody. I thought maybe if I kept ignoring them they'd go away. I felt guilty for even questioning it. If God was real I was pretty much a terrible person for*

thinking that he wasn't. But the questions kept resurfacing. It got to the point where I was miserable inside and where I couldn't pray or read the Bible, and I avoided anything to do with God. It wasn't that I didn't want God, I just felt like he wasn't there, and if he was, he wouldn't care about me. I felt like life had no purpose.

One day my dad told me that a missionary family needed help back overseas. He encouraged me to consider GOING with them if I was interested. Without realizing it, I was praying—something I hadn't been able to do for a long time.

Those six months overseas were some of the most challenging, and, at the same time, wonderful days of my life. In a city with no electricity and running water, orphans on the street and a hot sun burning constantly upon you, life could be hard. But I also learned that sometimes the hardest days of your life are the best, because in those days you rely on Jesus more than ever — there's nothing or no one else to lean on. I didn't have my friends, my family, or any fun things I liked to do . . . but I had Jesus. I realized he was all I needed. There have been times I've doubted his existence or my faith since then (it's not like everything is "fixed" all the sudden). But like my friend once told me, I became stronger. And it was because of him.

Outsiders will be tempted to let finances, adversity, or even "themselves" stop the vision God has given them. In 2 Timothy 4:5, Paul reminds his mentee Timothy to *"endure suffering . . . fulfill your ministry."* As if Paul were saying, "Keep going Outside Timothy! Share the message of hope in Jesus." A commitment such as Timothy's is transcendent and inspirational. Outsiders need to simply keep trusting God.

TAKE ACTION

As you think of your time to leave, be ready to ask yourself these questions:

- Are you already thinking of when you get to leave before you have started? Is this healthy?
- Have you given yourself fully to the calling Outside yet? What is holding you back? What does your vision look like years from now? Describe some obstacles you will have to overcome to get there.
- A paint store entrepreneur, homeowner, a school principal, a businessman, and a restaurateur came alongside a vision to help provide the needed space for our journey Outside—money wasn't the priority focus. Authenticity and clear vision motivated everyone to play their role. Make a list of those you can invite alongside you to help.

And looking intently at the council, Paul said, "Brothers, I have lived my life before God in all good conscience up to this day."
Acts 23:1

DON'T LET THE DOOR HIT YOU ON THE WAY OUT (LITERALLY)

One random Friday, when I was in my early twenties, things got really depressing.

In my mind, life had been one big fictionalized fairytale and it was getting difficult to maintain this false reality. Just out of college, my subconscious goal had been to keep moving fast enough and keep plenty of "fun" stuff planned, so I wouldn't have to deal with the hard questions. Mentally, I was exhausted and my body was full of anxiety.

Then it happened. "Are you sure you want *me* to go?" I stammered.

"Oh, I'm sure," said the youth pastor.

Perhaps this dude didn't know about my life. Sure, I had been coming back to church a bit, but Friday nights were still mine. (Oh, and Saturday too.)

But this youth pastor had planned a trip and was insistent that he wanted me to go. But, naturally, he didn't just want me to go to be the "fun guy." *No.* He wanted me to be a mentor. *Sheeeeew.*

I hadn't been to a church event outside of Sunday in years. It sounded super constraining and my flesh screamed, "No!" But for some reason, before I could really think about it, I hesitantly said, "Sure, I'll go."

What did I just do and how can I get out of this? How will I explain this to my buddies when they call me about Friday night and I'm at a church event? Searching, I quickly justified my thinking by the fact it was a trip to the beach.

When we got there, my old self was alive and well. When the kids had certain activities to choose from, called tracts, I created my own–Tract Lee. It was some time for me, myself, and the beach. When the kids got rambunctious, I talked to them like I talked to my college fraternity brothers, being careful to not use too many inappropriate words or phrases. The other mentors from different youth groups looked at me like I was highly unqualified and misplaced. I can remember one of them walking by saying, "God have mercy on their souls."

"You will know that forgiveness has begun when you recall those who hurt you and feel the power to wish them well."
– Lewis B. Smedes

Each night the entire camp had worship and teaching from the Bible, it couldn't be avoided. However, every evening when the call to worship came around, it felt abnormally liberating and I started to look forward to that time. I didn't want to run. I started to pick up the Bible.

I didn't know where the specific books in the Bible were located, and recalled scanning the table of contents to find the gospel of John. Maybe I played off my lack of Bible knowledge well, but if people noticed they didn't judge. That seemed different then the way my "friends" treated each other. I was a bit embarrassed but increasingly intrigued.

The night before we left, my old mentality started to shift. The freedom of this new life was calling my name. That's when I stumbled upon this passage:

Therefore, if anyone is in Christ, the new creation has come: The old has gone, the new is here! (2 Corinthians 5:17 NIV).

Could it be? In Jesus, I was finding that my old life was slipping away. I didn't have to clean it out and up. That He would do all of that for me. *Was I willing to let Him?* The old wasn't good enough and I needed to experience the newness found in Jesus.

As the youth group gathered at the end of the evening to debrief what we had learned, that same youth pastor looked at me and said, "Lee, how's it going for you?" One last time, my mind wondered if I could run, so I sized up the carpeted wall divider on wheels and wondered if I could blow through it. But, I realized what was on the other side—the same old same. So, again, without making myself ready, "I said, I need to refocus my life on Jesus. I admit it. I need to surrender." The place erupted. The entire youth group piled on me. Once they were pulled back off, they gathered around and prayed for me.

On that long bus ride home, I knew I was in over my head. There was so much I needed to release and so many changes that were going to come. I also knew some of my friends were going to absolutely hammer me.

To be a catalyst for change, you will leave something or someone behind. Inside is full of places and people who don't want to "Go Out." It's part of the deal. For the Outsider, it might be a friend, an employer, a family member, or a work colleague that rises up to challenge your new life. They will doubt your sincerity and motives. They will remind you of the old life, as if you needed any help. Here's a truth all Outsiders need to know before they start:

You can't say "Hello" to something new without properly saying "Goodbye" to the old.

How you "leave" and go Outside, communicates much about your integrity and the legitimacy of your calling. Did you leave unannounced? Did you take off? Didn't get your way? For you, it was time to prove the world wrong. Did you leave angry? Is your vision rooted in bitterness, self-interest, or competitiveness?

Hold up.

"See to it that no one fails to obtain the grace of God; that no "root of

bitterness" springs up and causes trouble, and by it many become defiled" (Hebrews 12:15).

Let's be honest. Bitterness is a spiritual poison. This isn't a good foundation. Most definitely not a good way to start something new. Sure, "holy frustration" has spurred many great works, but rooted rancor always will come back to bite an Outsider. The initial driver wears off and the foundational characteristics of animosity show through. It could be years later, but the shadow is cast and resentment will burn you down in the end.

OK. I got it, but how do I get started in this new Outsider life?

1. Don't forget, when you trust in Jesus, Jesus has you. He won't leave you. Ever. His grace is the sustaining factor for your salvation and future. No matter what happens, you're a child of God. That's winning enough. When the persecution comes, count it as affirmation for doing the right thing in Him. Check out Deuteronomy 31:6 and Philippians 1:12-26.

2. Consider the Costs. Jesus said, *"No one who puts a hand to the plow and looks back is fit for service in the kingdom of God"* (Luke 9:60-62 NIV).

3. Don't be afraid to offer apologies or forgiveness first. If the reaction isn't what you wanted or expected, just let it go. Years later, the way you left the past will speak volumes about your character today. *"But do this in a gentle and respectful way. Keep your conscience clear. Then if people speak against you, they will be ashamed when they see what a good life you live because you belong to Christ"* (I Peter 3:16 NLT).

4. Get ready, because as an Outsider, others you have invited to go with you might leave you too. Always do your best to say goodbye well, and as you go, always do your best to keep the door open for others.

5. Fight bitterness and don't go negative, it will send you sideways. Keep at the work God has given you to do.

"Let all bitterness and wrath and anger and clamor and slander be put away from you, along with all malice. Be kind to one another, tenderhearted, forgiving one another, as God in Christ forgave you" (Ephesians 4:31-32).

TAKE ACTION

- Is there a person in your life who never gave you a chance? Are you still carrying the anger and frustration of others not believing in you? What will you do?
- Before you start your first steps Outside, take time to allow God to illuminate areas of reconciliation needed in your life.
- Recognize the difference between conviction and guilt. Don't allow feelings of shame stop you from going forward. Remember Romans 8:1.
- Get advice from a trusted mentor about your old and new life. How will you stay in community as you start your new life Outside?

KEEP OUT

Growing up I can recall my father, Alton Webb, being very active around the house. I can also remember him eating weird things like "milk cake"—which is cake in a cup with milk poured over it. (Actually pretty delicious.) If anything needed attention, he was on it. Chopping wood, hanging blinds, helping with homework, or coaching our rec team—Dad was there. My mother and he were both very consistent. Every Saturday night, Mom would watch television sitcoms and eat popcorn with my brother, sister, and me while Dad worked on his Sunday school lesson at the kitchen table.

As consistent as Dad was, he was also a risk taker and starter of multiple businesses. He'd always encourage me, "If you don't risk anything, it won't be worth anything." He refused to let things remain static. Dad made a living not allowing things to settle or appealing to the industry standard. My father taught me much about going Outside.

In 2001, we built an office building in our small community. It was in an area that was less developed and offered (in condominium fashion) the flexibility to sell or lease the units. Turns out, the market was ready for space. It was a great project. Dad looked at me and said, "Okay, time to build another one." Instead, I was nervous and ready to retreat. He continued, "It would be a shame if we didn't do more after all we went through—I think the market could handle more." I refused.

It's true. Not long after you start, you'll want a break. *After all, didn't you just take a huge step?* It seems to be working, now . . . let's just take a breath. Yes, all of us need proper rest. Get some, but be ready to *go* again. A movement that doesn't keep going forward can head the wrong way—back inside. Something started with an Outside vision has to stay Outside and keep Outside. If not, it "grows back."

So, what does "growing back" look like?

- Declining to create an invitation and the space for new people.
- Refusing fresh perspective.
- Sliding along instead of pioneering.
- Going without asking the hard questions.
- Ignoring problems.
- Hoarding leadership.
- Keeping it to a few instead of multiplying.
- Burning out leaders.
- Reluctance to plan for the future.
- Allowing opportunities to slip away because of indecisiveness.
- Trusting your own logic instead of allowing faith in God to lead.

By refusing to build alongside my father, I allowed the mission we had together to grow backwards. What happened? Other investors started constructing office complexes too. The park where we initiated new office product, would become a real destination.

We still have the joy of stepping Outside together. We took a risk, and it went well. But I learned that I wasn't ready to keep going when I needed to. I told God, "Look how far I've come and all that we've been through!" He whispered back, *"Trust in me with all your heart, don't lean on your own understanding. Acknowledge me in all your ways, and I will make straight your paths"* (Proverbs 3:5-6). A missed chance, but I learned that to be a true Outsider, I would need to *stay Outside.*

What will you do when the opportunity to grow is evident?

What will you do when you realize the non-profit you lead can help more people than just a few?

What will you do when your waiting room is packed?

What will you do when that difficult personnel situation arises?

What will you do when your social media becomes stagnate?

What will you do when orders come in and you can't fill them?

What will you do if life or health circumstances prevent you from being in charge?

As Outsiders, it's our job to keep leading and Going Outside, and we have to encourage others who are part of our shared vision to do the same. If not, we run the risk of becoming Insiders. The vision becomes stale and people start voting with their feet—right out the door.

"If you profess to go outside the camp, others will look for something extra in you,—mind that they are not disappointed. They ought to expect it, and I am glad they do expect it."
—Charles Spurgeon

Bobby and Sue Andriot had a vision years ago for downtown development in the community they loved. They saw a window to make a difference. Their vision compelled them to revitalize numerous buildings, some that were infested with drugs and crime, and others that just needed some good old fashioned love.

Small towns across America are desperate for revitalization and need places for local people to connect. Restaurants can offer that environment. However, according to entrepreneur.com, 61 percent of restaurants fail within the first three years.[11] It's a risky idea for most. *But*, it wasn't for Bobby and Sue. After decades of owning successful businesses and experiencing the ups and downs of entrepreneurship (it ain't all cotton candy, y'all), they decided against retirement.

After buying and improving many locations over the years, they turned their attention to a dilapidated historic building. Although the old place was desperate for help, their vision would make it become a thriving Italian restaurant. Not only is it quite delicious; it is also an example of community stewardship and a success story, despite the odds. Bobby and Sue couldn't stay inside. They teach many about God's faithfulness and how He has enabled them to stay Outside.

TAKE ACTION

- Read John 15:1-8. Outline what you think it takes to sustainably stay Outside.
- In order to stay Outside, you have to continually prepare for the future. What are you doing today to be ready to reinvest in people and resources five years from now?

"Save more than you spend, but do not hoard. Reinvest. Grow. Focus on re-plowing your fields so they bear fruit."
– Jennifer Ritchie Payette

SQUAD
GOALS

Anxiety filled the air. Not only was it an extremely humid day in the summer of 2009, but our family room was completely packed. I took a deep breath, and thought, *this has to be said or the vision will die a slow death.* I opened my mouth and the air left the room, "This is happening folks. We want to open the church to the public on 10-10-10. Smiles came on the faces of many. Some of those smiles would fade when I said, "Now, you have to decide. Are you in or out?" To this point, the risk had been all on Rachel and me. As the reality of what we were doing settled in the room, they looked down, up, and everywhere but at me.

Leaders with an Outside focus must invite others Outside with them. Inviting others starts in the beginning, but becomes vital as the journey goes forward. Although modest leaders are reluctant to ask others for anything, they know a movement won't move without others involved.

The struggle will be real when you head Outside. Rachel and I had a real sense of partnership together through small business and community involvement. We mutually supported my leadership of a church plant. There have been many times where we have questioned our decision to step out. We've struggled with perceptions of others. During the initial phase of the church plant, we heard questions and comments like: "What are you doing?!" and "That has to be hard, we've been thinking of your poor little family." or the indirect assault on our parenting, "Is this the best thing for your kids?" Sometimes we just wanted to go back inside.

We entered Outside together with sincere trust of each other. Going Outside is not worth losing your family—keep them first. Commit together. Draw ridiculously broad lines to protect each other. Family is the main ingredient to your future team.

An extension of your personal family includes a team of mentors, fellow committed and called participants, encouragers, and helpers. These people are your launch team.

Choose your team members wisely. Good team members have respectable character. They aren't necessarily the most popular, highly educated, or most experienced. I've found that the best ones spend time with God.

> "When they saw the courage of Peter and John and realized that they were unschooled, ordinary men, they were astonished and they took note that these men had been with Jesus."
> Acts 4:13 (NIV)

Good team members aren't perfect, but they stand in the gap. They understand commitment and forgiveness. Your team is best if its members are different than you. They don't question you to death, but will still happily speak up. They remain flexible to God's plan and His movement. The best teams are transparent. They still get nervous, but have a positive attitude. They aren't harsh. They are willing, enthusiastic and understand that developing good vision can be a process of small steps.

You may not know that you've chosen the best squad until after you've left your role as leader. Give the team opportunity to lead early on; they will be the future vision carriers after you are gone. They are future Outsiders.

Here is a story from Wes Keene, a member of our team:

> *"God what are You calling me to do?" Little did I know, He was calling me to be part of a church plant. At the time of joining the launch team I didn't even know what a church plant was. All I realized at the time was that God had called a specific group of folks with different personalities, different backgrounds and upbringings. Different gifts and talents, different church experiences. There were no 'know-it-all's.' There was no "we can't do that," and there was no worrying about "what if we fail?" I think we all felt the Lord's hand in everything that we were doing, and I think we kept our eyes on him as he lead us. I grew more spiritually in those few months leading up to our first open gathering on 10-10-10 than I ever had. That time solidified and simplified my relationship with Jesus. I had a front row seat as God built a modern day ark right here in our community.*
>
> *Now as exciting as it was to be on the launch team, it was not easy. For me and my family there was an adjustment period. Prior to that, we were involved with church but weren't necessarily committed. We went on most Sundays, and would volunteer occasionally as our schedules allowed. It was time to change from just being involved to being 'all in.' That was tough at times for me, because I would be needed in a particular area, and I'd want to retreat or come up with an excuse to get out of it. But by only doing what was asked and trusting in God, I was rewarded by seeing others encouraged and challenged to do the same.*
>
> *What was great about it? Everything! We didn't just talk about Going Outside, we were where the action was. I loved the comment from one of our members, "At*

other churches I'm a scandal; here I'm a story!"
    *It's important for your starting team to have a heart
and a desire to be a part of change. Not all of those
folks look or think alike.*

You'll need lots of help to go Outside. If the vision is legit, it will grow beyond your personal ability to maintain it. Plus, amazing things happen when leaders don't care who gets the credit!

Martin Luther King, Jr. had a dream and a vision that wouldn't be subdued. Quoting Amos 5:24, in his "I Have a Dream Speech" Dr. King said, "No, no, we are not satisfied, and we will not be satisfied until justice rolls down like waters, and righteousness like a mighty stream." Dr. King had a plan to actualize his vision through nonviolence and demonstration. He was a true Outsider—a great example of casting and protecting a compelling vision. Jo Ann Robinson said of the team of people inspired by the leadership of Martin Luther King Jr., "The amazing thing about our movement is that it is a protest of the people. It is not a one-man show. It is not a preacher's show. It's the people. The masses of this town, who are tired of being trampled on, are responsible. The leaders couldn't stop it if they wanted to."[12]

Your squad is critical. If you don't know the answer, you can't be afraid to ask someone who does. Build your team and consider these three types of people:

- Mentor(s) are indispensable—especially when you get stuck. This isn't someone to take over, but rather someone to help you think through issues regularly with purpose. They are always ready for your phone call or request for dinner. In your journey together, you will sort through questions and confusion, talk about discomfort and celebrate lots of wins. You'll be able to share emotions candidly and receive acceptance in return. A favorite saying from one of our mentors is "The key to the journey is to focus one day at a time, rest in Him and be faithful in word, action and attitude."

    o On a professional level, find qualified people to help you think through a system for financials in your organization. How will you handle money? What operational systems do you need in place? Who is someone that has legitimate experience in that arena? Will you need written policies or procedures? What about regulatory requirements? There will be several professionals you need depending on your circumstances—don't minimize their wisdom and skip steps to save money or time.

- A detail person – a good note taker, someone who can hold the administrative and communication pieces together. It's someone who can remind you, ask questions, and goes with you on this journey. As an Outsider, this is probably not your strength. Find someone to help you.

- Apprenticeship is vastly important. Outsiders don't have the many structures in place when starting—that's just fine. But a system of training a new generation of Outsiders is a vital piece of mission sustainability. On the job training and accompanying other Outsiders is the best way to multiply more Outsiders. Include an apprentice early and always leave an empty chair for a new one.

Going Outside is best when done in community. Many an Outsider has tried to head Outside without anyone else and found it couldn't and shouldn't be done alone.

Going solo is not consistent with the nature of the God who calls us out. God, the Creator of all things, is eternally existent in three persons: Father, Son, and Holy Spirit. Out of His Trinitarian love and example for us, God sets the standard for us to be in community with and for one another. Being sent, supported, and encouraged by a local faith family is indispensable for the Outsider.

I should have known, but I now realize my beginning vision wasn't just a personal vision, but God's vision. I learned that going Outside is to do something for others, not just me. That's much different than just plain ol' starting something. It's a mindset and a realization of where real endurance and lasting things are found.

As an Outsider, you realize early in your adventure, "I can't do everything!" You have a choice to make. Get others engaged on a higher level or sink. Hoard leadership or invite others to spur the vision ahead. There's really no middle ground.

While the answer to get others involved is simple logic, it is much harder in practice. When Outsiders start something, we hold it closely and tightly. Every detail and decision is ours. Our leadership fists are clinched. In the name of insuring quality and success, we control it completely. It's understandable and why not? Who else is going to do it anyway?

Reinforcements are the extra personnel or reserve sent to increase support in sustainable ways, and during my initial years of leading business and ministry related activities, I didn't understand the importance of reinforcement. Like most, I was domineering and monitored everything. It stressed me out. But, I had to let go.

As I started to dream beyond my egocentric approach, I took a risk. I wouldn't shirk my responsibilities, but as God sent me help, I gave some tasks away. When it didn't turn out like I expected, I didn't worry about it. This mentality actually became quite addictive. Empowering others to grow in their leadership became my favorite part of the day. In fact, giving more to others increased their capacity to go further, grow faster, and it provided space for me to concentrate on using my gifts best.

We've had some good examples of reinforcement in history. George Washington gave away his newfound power and leadership twice. Once as general and another time as president. Robert Frost said about the Father of America, "I often say of George Washington that he was one of the few in the whole history of the world who was not carried away by power." Isn't that the idea?

How many leaders have held a post of leadership for decades and not given any of it away? When the time comes for them to retire or they find something better, the remaining sad souls in the organization look around at each other. They've been left high and dry.

Outsiders think bigger. Outsiders lead like every day could be their last. When they start, they don't place timetables on their departure. Some will stay for decades before their time to leave; others might be more short term. But, they ask questions that seem alien to insiders like, "How I am setting this up for the next leader? Who can I invest in now, that will take my place when my time comes? "Who's *going* next?"

Outsiders have right motives and desire to be a part of starting a real movement instead of a self-centered success. They underpin the DNA of the vision by inviting new leaders from the beginning and as they leave.

The former pastor of Southeast Christian Church, Bob Russell, is a mentor and someone I respect deeply. Bob writes in his book *Transition Plan*, "Very few churches are actively engaged in discussion about crafting a plan for transitioning before their pastor's announced departure."[13]

In my role as a church leader, committed to multiplication, not planning for succession seemed like a fatal mistake. Even if I didn't know the timing or the "who," I wanted to be proactive and optimistic about a smooth transition.

When Blake Lawyer came on staff at our church, our leaders knew he was a talented and hard-working individual with good character. As he and I journeyed together for over a year serving our congregation, I began to realize that even though we really liked each other, we were different leaders and processed decisions quite uniquely. In my head, I found myself saying, "He's going to be a good leader, but not the leader of leaders, he's too different from me." How prideful! Still learning, my eyes were opened by something else Bob wrote, "The successor should not be a clone."

After several years in leadership and ministry growth, I knew the church was moving from an *out there* idea to having a real future. For others the timing of a calling might go on for decades, but for some reason I sensed my time as leader was winding down.

In my fourth year, I mapped out a potential succession plan while continuing to watch Blake and other leaders grow. It was exciting. Blake took on more responsibility and even became a teacher on Sunday mornings. I began to wonder even more, but waited for God's timing.

Another leader and I were talking about the growth of Blake and he asked me a question. "Do you use summer tires in the winter?" I thought, *hmmm*. Then it hit me. Different seasons require different leaders. Was the time here? I deliberated on verses like 1 Peter 4:10, *"As each has received a gift, use it to serve one another, as good stewards of God's varied grace."*

Church participation had grown to over 300 people, tons of kids, eight ministry partners, 13 community groups and new people connecting each week. Blake shared fresh perspective for the new upcoming year and I was admittedly getting tired. It had started to affect my attitude and leadership. I was concerned for my family and the church. I wondered, "Am I helping this go forward or holding it back?"

After a strategy meeting for the upcoming year, I asked Blake, "Who do you think needs to lead the future? Are you ready to be that leader?" He confidently and humbly answered, "Yes." My response, "You don't know how happy I am to hear that!" Experience Blake's story:

> *I remember the inner turmoil that came with knowing*
> *deep down I was more about myself than the God I*

was serving. I had treated my leadership positions in church like stepping stones - but would never admit that. It was during days that I was struggling with being more content that I received a call about joining Christ Community Church's team. Maybe this was it. This might be the opportunity I had been waiting for. It was a long journey from that first phone call to the Sunday morning that I would transition into the role as lead pastor. Along the way I would learn that it wasn't the opportunity that needed to change, it was me.

Only by God's grace, I made a decision in the middle of that transition to do something I hadn't previously done—be sold out in following the leader. Instead of nit picking or second guessing, I was going to follow to the best of my ability. I failed in following, more often than not, in the name of improvement and control. But each time, as I returned to following the leader, I found a clearer picture of what the God I was serving wanted to do.

My critical spirit had to learn how to hope—to believe the best about a situation before it seemed believable.

I'll never forget the Sunday that I understood how to serve and lead something bigger than myself. Our story that day was to be told by a Hispanic lady who had considered abortion, but decided against it after visiting our local pregnancy center. She was to tell her story and introduce the daughter who was alive because of what God changed in her!

My excitement drained away when they showed up minutes before the beginning of the service and informed that the little girl had brought a CD and was prepared to sing. I panicked. This was not on my schedule. With no time to practice, there was no way to know what was going to happen. I had no control. Just as I was about to shut down the request, Lee swooped in and with excitement on his face told them how much he was looking forward to her singing.

I could have cussed.

Thirty minutes and thirty gallons of sweat later, I joined every person in that school in one of the few standing ovations I've ever witnessed at Christ Community Church. From that moment on, the inner turmoil of serving myself faded away into the responsibility of leading with hope for the best—wherever God would have me!

When I became pastor, it was never about my ability to make it better or a desire to seize control. It was about my learning to follow. If I had never been able to follow Lee, I would have never been able to follow God with the zeal it requires to lead something so much bigger than myself.

The concept of reinforcing is the scariest thing you'll do. After all, you've started something that is conceivably wrapped up in your identity. What will happen to you? What will you do when you leave? What will happen to the organization?

You'll learn that the reinforcing process requires more faith than when you first went Outside. In the end, your investment in others and willingness to step away will demonstrate whether you have started something "beyond" or merely something "good," that is ultimately all about you. Don't worry. Your work won't be forgotten and you'll always be a part of it, even if you aren't physically there.

When you initiate the work, make your goal to look back in healthy ways and watching others grow. What if one day you look around to see others leading the vision further without you in the room? That could be your greatest reward.

TAKE ACTION

- Read Matthew 10:1-42, 11:1, and Luke 10:1-24. List the ways Jesus empowered the disciples along their way together. List the ways your leadership can model Jesus, beginning from the first day you start.
- If an external minded leader waits until the end to drum up reinforcements, it's too late. How will you prevent this?
- Who have you empowered to lead beyond yourself? Start now by giving ownership to others based on their gifts.
- How are you helping others take the vision to new levels without having to be in control?

NOT THE CONCLUSION

THE GREAT
COMMISSION

The same pit I had in my stomach the Sunday we walked out
of church was coming back again. For us, it had been months
of eye-opening and affirming occurrences since we initially told
our church family what was happening in our hearts. We had
prayed, cried, laughed with excitement, and in the end knew
our hearts were being prepared for this journey.

After talking with church leaders, we all decided it was a
good time to give them an update. Even though nothing had
formally started yet, we were confident in our call to go Outside
and plant a new church. But, we knew we couldn't go without
the sending and reinforcement of our church family.

As we walked into the church that humid day, we were still
scratching our heads. *How could we leave this place?* We were full
of joy to be following Jesus, but it didn't make sense logically. As
expected, those same friendly faces welcomed us to the chapel.
As I nervously stepped to the small podium, I could feel my face
flushing red—again.

The deacons and staff graciously gave me the floor and listened intently as I shared the vision for going Outside. I started
with my story as a child in that building. I shared with them my
deep gratitude to Mrs. Burge, my first Sunday school teacher,
and my appreciation for the countless investments so many of

them had poured into my life. (I also stopped briefly to apologize for the many times I raised the blood pressure of more than one youth leader.)

I recalled a deep memory of trusting Christ as Savior and being baptized at twelve, followed by years of playing cards, eating candy, and half-listening to Bible studies with a handful of high school classmates on Sundays and Wednesday nights. Most of the people around the room had watched me grow up.

When I left for college, I stopped attending church altogether, but that didn't stop those same leaders from welcoming me back on summer breaks and after graduation. After spending time with the youth pastor, Jay, who happened to be my age, they were able to see my life transform once again as I made the decision to live out the faith that I first embraced when I was twelve years old. They cheered me on as I explored my identity as a twenty-something building a relationship with God, even giving me full support to use the church building and resources to start a ministry for other college and post-college students who were at the same (sometimes overlooked and awkward) phase of church life. They celebrated with me as I dated and married Rachel, followed by the joy they shared with our family as we welcomed and dedicated our first baby in the church.

The fact is, my family foundation in Christ was strongly rooted and established there. All those memories and happenings were enough for a lifetime, but they were also the very reason I couldn't stay. It was time for me to go.

As we shared the vision for a new work God was doing, we leaned into the fact that only 13% of the people that lived in our community attended church. Our belief was that a new kind of church, married to the same truth, could help reach the other 87%. We shared our missional focus of serving the city, building relationships, sharing our story and the story of Jesus. It seemed the logic to stay was disappearing for everyone in the room. People Outside needed God's love and we had to go.

Tears flowed.

We were pumped when they encouraged us deeply and unanimously supported our efforts. Then they huddled around us and prayed over us for this "monumental task." It wasn't like we were leaving town to start a new congregation—we were actually staying in the *same* small town. Not allowing competition to be a dividing force, we joined together into what we all believed God was calling us do. Sure, it was confusing at times and we didn't have all the answers, but we all had our faith and trust in each other.

I had already learned so much and we hadn't even started.

But it was time to start.

Almost, immediately upon going Outside, we realized how comfortable we were on those easy Sunday mornings. We could just show up and look forward to our big brunch and long naps afterward on Sunday afternoon.

All of a sudden, we didn't even have a name of our church much less our own building. But Outside is for the *birds*.

As God opened up doors and windows, we and so many others kept working hard. Fueled by the compassion of Jesus, eventually we were able to have weekly worship gatherings. Since we didn't have a permanent building, it was lots of work each week. Our team would faithfully unload and load a trailer to get things set. We used a sound system that would go haywire randomly, but we were stoked to even have one.

More importantly, we had to learn how to minister to people. The poor and hurting. *How would we help people get food? How would we help the homeless find shelter? What about those struggling with addiction or going through a painful time?* I was called to go to the hospital to visit people, which always made me uneasy, even if it was for a new baby arriving! I did a wedding and then led a service at a funeral. *Phew.*

I was starting to understand the grind of truly caring for people when they needed it, not just when I wanted to do so or when I just so happened to pass by them in a church hallway on Sunday. Some times people would come help us serve and other times, people would come to a gathering and say, "This ain't for me." Yet, many times people, who had never gone to church, would come, stay, and get plugged in. That was such a thrill. To see their lives changed by Jesus—one person at a time. It made it all worth it!

When the church pros (not that they even exist for real) would come and tell us what we were doing wrong, we'd smile and say, "That's okay, but we're going to keep going Outside!" Our vision was Outside-focused and it drove us to even serving on Sunday mornings instead of staying inside for worship. The reactions of newcomers on these days were priceless. Some would say, "That's great—where are we going?" For other people, you'd sometimes turn around and they would have already left. No worries. We understood.

•••

Just as I had shared the story of my calling with my former church family, we would continue to encourage others to share their story too. From the very beginning of our weekly church gathering for worship (and even in our home groups), someone shared their story (or in Churchology, their "testimony," but of course being difficult, we never use that terminology). This method gave us the feeling of an AA meeting. Sharing stories promoted the heart and vision of going Outside. Even today, it gives people ownership and puts them in a situation where they have to get uncomfortable. It helps people practice for real life scenarios. When God calls them to share at the grocery store, school pick-up line, while having coffee, or at their job.

As a pastor, I didn't care if someone went a little long or didn't say the words in the ever-elusive language of Churchology. Sometimes people would talk for only thirty seconds. It didn't matter. We encouraged people to just be "who you are and tell people what Jesus has done and is doing in your life now." Sure, they would mess up, have to start over, and begin to cry, but in these moments of raw truthfulness, it promoted a movement of authenticity in our local body of believers. Everyday people shared everyday stories about how Jesus changed their lives.

It felt groundbreaking. It made real impact. But it was just people being people.

Some pastors would have been extremely reluctant and are too hesitant to allow this. *What if someone shares their opinion or eats into the sermon time or is too transparent?* It's funny, because in my mind, these things were non-negotiables for our faith community. It helped us prepare our hearts to learn from the teaching of God's word that followed—especially as we had communion together each week. It helped us to deepen relationships and share in the messiness of life *for real*.

At the end of the gathering people stuck around. Some of them huddled in small groups, others laughed and talked, some pondered and prayed, and others trusted in Jesus for the first time. It was evident the Holy Spirit was present and working. It was about the journey Outside together. In light of the grace Jesus had shown us and reminded us of each week, what would be our next step? Where was Jesus calling us to go Outside with our time and influence? How would Jesus change our story for the glory of His?

Our heart as a little church plant was for the capital-C Church to give permission to everyday folks—to allow people to share their story. So, we started sharing the story of what God was doing in our church with other churches in our area. We partnered with other churches and ministries, then we allowed them to share their story in our setting. It was radical, but not to us.

We believed that this was important for people to do on a person-to-person basis. That we, as the capital-C Church , needed to teach people to listen to people's stories, share their story, and understand how it intersects with gospel truth. It was simple. Plus, it overlapped with daily activity—it wasn't a new program that cost any money, had to be built, or another thing to put on your calendar. We stopped trying to place people into boxes, timetables, and organized groups with specified discussion questions. We didn't have to box it up and summarize the outcome each week with a posted attendance board. It has to be gritty, challenging, and profoundly encouraging, because that is when God truly get's the glory. The "win" for the capital-C Church is not that numerically more people attend, but that one person shared their one story so that lives can be changed on an individual basis and the world can start seeing what the gospel really looks like. This relational approach grew our church and helped us participate in the shared mission Jesus gives us to tell others about His life changing story:

How, then, can they call on the one they have not believed in? And how can they believe in the one of whom they have not heard? And how can they hear without someone preaching to them? And how can anyone preach unless they are sent? As it is written: "How beautiful are the feet of those who bring good news" Romans 10:14-15 (NIV).

As our particular church grew and grew and grew, so did the Church. More and more people felt the calling to go Outside and be a part of what the early Church and God Himself, commanded. Because, guess what? The Church was never called to stay put. The Church was, by definition, the assembly of people called out by Jesus.

The early church demonstrated sending people out of the church, not as something only the crazy people in the church did (*ahem*), but as an act of reacting to the Holy Spirit's leading. Sharing the Gospel is not for someone else to do; it's for all of us to do—and you don't need the four walls of a church to do it. Think about it. Christ and His disciples didn't have any preconceived walls and we shouldn't either. We all just need to go Outside with our everyday lives.

When the apostles in Jerusalem heard that Samaria had accepted the word of God, they sent Peter and John to Samaria (Acts 8:14).

Together, the church we were called out of and the new church God was starting was forming and doing the work of *the* Church. Together, we were given a commission—to be stewards of something much bigger than ourselves—to come together and be the body of the greatest Outsider their ever was. The Church can't help but join Him in the action, where He has called us—to the ends of the earth. And there is no one who embodied the body of the church better than the one who gave Himself for it.

So after they had fasted and prayed, they placed their hands on them and sent them off.
Acts 13:3

JESUS, THE ULTIMATE OUTSIDER

The entire passage of Hebrews 13:11-15 jumped out at me like a roaring lion. It was the summation of my life in a simplistic, yet tragically profound way. Why tragic? There's part of the passage I couldn't run pass or gloss over. It was just two words. "Jesus suffered."

Torture. Unspeakable Shame. Degradation. Crucifixion. The severity of it all.

I needed time to contemplate the agony Jesus went through for me. It was worth deep reflection. He took all my wickedness, my unkind words and acts, my depravity, and sin, upon Himself. Not just a little bit until it hurt, but all of it. In fact, Jesus took the sin of the whole world—not just mine. A completely unbearable thought, but a vastly heroic and motivating call to action.

"For even the Son of Man did not come to be served, but to serve, and to give his life as a ransom for many" Mark 10:45 (NIV).

Jesus Christ was and is the ultimate Outsider. He left His heavenly home of luxury to enter a world filled with sin. He loved us all too much to just stay put at home. Jesus was and is the only one who could make our wrongs right. He put Himself aside and went Outside on a mission to rescue humanity.

For I delivered to you as of first importance what I also received: that

Christ died for our sins in accordance with the Scriptures, that he was buried, that he was raised on the third day in accordance with the Scriptures (1 Corinthians 15:3-4).

The journey Outside for Jesus started in humble beginnings. Born in a manger among animals and soon to be sought after, not only by people who wanted to worship Him as King, but by a king who wanted to kill Him. Later, Jesus was baptized and then in miraculous fashion the "Spirit of God descended like a dove and rested on Him" (Matthew 3:16).

People started following Jesus. He invited others to join Him and people began to trust in Jesus and His teachings. In Him, they have found the promised Messiah. He changed water into wine and drove the money changers out of the temple. Jesus traveled Outside intentionally through places that the strict legalists would never go. He mingled with outcasts, ate meals with crooks and sinners, and uplifted women in a time when tradition would have forbidden such an act. He healed the blind, lame, and paralyzed when others would have passed them by. Jesus fed thousands of hungry people, walked on water, washed feet, and allowed the children to come to Him when others thought He was too busy.

As the ultimate Outsider, Jesus did things that only He could do. He took the seemingly lofty occasion and used it to call out hypocrisy, while pointing to truth, time and time again.

> *One Sabbath, when he went to dine at the house of a ruler of the Pharisees, they were watching him carefully. And behold, there was a man before him who had dropsy. And Jesus responded to the lawyers and Pharisees, saying, "Is it lawful to heal on the Sabbath, or not?" But they remained silent. Then he took him and healed him and sent him away. And he said to them, "Which of you, having a son or an ox that has fallen into a well on a Sabbath day, will not immediately pull him out?" And they could not reply to these things.*
> *He said also to the man who had invited him,*

"When you give a dinner or a banquet, do not invite your friends or your brothers or your relatives or rich neighbors, lest they also invite you in return and you be repaid. But when you give a feast, invite the poor, the crippled, the lame, the blind, and you will be blessed, because they cannot repay you. For you will be repaid at the resurrection of the just" (Luke 14:1-6,12-14).

Despite our shortcomings, Jesus was (and still is) determined to show every one of us His love. When people deserted Him, he kept *going*. Jesus brought the dead back to life and would continually beat back fear to comfort those who were mourning. He prayed earnestly for people.

As Jesus continued to head Outside, others focused on inside things. His compassion got Him arrested, yet he had no wrong doings. Jesus was denied by close friends and experienced injustice on the most historic levels. He was flogged, mocked, and beaten. Even more astonishing was His unwillingness to care for Himself. At any moment, He could at once call down legions of angels to do battle for Him (Matthew 26:53). Nope. Jesus surrendered Himself fully, died the most horrific death by hanging on a cross until His work was completely finished.

For Jesus, Outside was literally "Outside." His crucifixion happened Outside the gates of the city in the same place where animal sacrifices were burned in smoldering fire. Then and now, Outside is a disgustingly unclean place. As we read in the Old Testament, *"And the bull for the sin offering and the goat for the sin offering, whose blood was brought in to make atonement in the Holy Place, shall be carried outside the camp. Their skin and their flesh and their dung shall be burned up with fire"* (Leviticus 16:27).

Not only was "outside" the unclean place for animal sacrifice remains, it was also the desolate place where unclean people were forced to stay.

"The leprous person who has the disease shall wear torn clothes and let the hair of his head hang loose, and he shall cover his upper lip and cry out, 'Unclean, unclean.' He shall remain unclean as long as he has the disease.

He is unclean. He shall live alone. His dwelling shall be outside the camp."
Leviticus 13:45-46

The mission to clean the unclean was resolved in Jesus when He came for our rescue. Being the ultimate Outsider would prove the most demanding journey ever recorded in human history. Only the Son of God could do it with perfection. He would end the need for our workings and sacrifices; once and for all. We are all unclean, but Jesus would end the need for us to be alone in the shadows ashamedly crying out, "Unclean, Unclean!"

"Cleanse me with hyssop, and I will be clean; wash me, and I will be whiter than snow" (Psalm 51:7 NIV).

In this dramatic Outsider path, He poured himself out for each of us (yes, you too), showed us the full extent of His love, defeated sin and conquered death by His resurrection.

That's good news.

Here's the stirring part. The same missionary God that sent Jesus, has invited us to join Him Outside. Empowered by his spirit and grace, believers of Jesus have been given a gift of salvation and one to live on mission worldwide. In our going Outside, we have the opportunity to reflect and bring our Creator glory through our everyday lives—one day at a time, and one person at a time.

Jesus replied, "Let us go somewhere else—to the nearby villages—so I can preach there also. That is why I have come."
Mark 1:38

With an external and eternal perspective, together, we the followers of Jesus, are all Outsiders. Sure, we might be everyday people, working the nine to five with kids and a ten o'clock bedtime, but with faith in an extraordinary God, we can see the world changed. I mean wasn't Christ oddly normal for being so divine? Check out this excerpt from James Allan Francis's

One Solitary Life:

> *Here is a man who was born in an obscure village, the child of a peasant woman.*
>
> *He grew up in another obscure village, where He worked in a carpenter shop until He was thirty, and then for three years He was an itinerant preacher.*
>
> *He never wrote a book. He never held an office. He never owned a home. He never had a family. He never went to college. He never put his foot inside a big city. He never traveled two hundred miles from the place where He was born. He never did one of the things that usually accompany greatness. He had no credentials but Himself. He had nothing to do with this world except the naked power of His divine manhood.*
>
> *While still a young man, the tide of public opinion turned against Him. His friends ran away. One of them denied Him. He was turned over to His enemies. He went through the mockery of a trial. He was nailed to a cross between two thieves. His executioners gambled for the only piece of property He had on earth while He was dying—and that was his coat.*
>
> *When he was dead He was taken down and laid in a borrowed grave through the pity of a friend. Nineteen wide centuries have come and gone and today He is the centerpiece of the human race and the leader of the column of progress.*
>
> *I am far within the mark when I say that all the armies that ever marched, and all the navies that ever were built, and all the parliaments that ever sat, all the kings that ever reigned, put together have not affected the life of man upon this earth as powerfully as has that One Solitary Life.*[14]

It's because of his perfect example of selflessness, that I could even consider my excitement of the outside world. It's also the reason I can't stay and I must go.

Remember, Jesus said, "Go" (Matthew 28:19 NIV).

TAKE ACTION

- Has Jesus changed your life?
- Can you change the Outside if you haven't been changed from within?
- Where will you find the strength to Go Outside?
- All our dreams and desires should ultimately point to the Ultimate Outsider—Jesus. What parts of your life are self-seeking instead of Jesus seeking?

Jesus Christ, you are the God whom we approach without pride, and before whom we humble ourselves without despair.
– Blaise Pascal

JOIN THE OUTSIDER MOVEMENT

So, now you know my story. I'm a Christ follower, husband, daddy, main street entrepreneur, church planter, small business owner, and I have a peculiar family nickname, Leedle. (At least that's the bio description on my twitter account for now.)

So, what am I up to now? Is this the conclusion or just the start of something? Good question.

First, I love being married to Rachel. That's for sure.

Second, I love being Daddy. It's so awesome to have the space to coach my children's rec teams and to watch Warren do back bridges at her gymnastics class.

Third, I love small business and entrepreneurship. Who knows where it will lead—but, for now I've got a business to run!

Fourth, what about ministry? After planting the church and stepping aside joyfully, it's been an honor to serve without a leadership title. For me, initiating the church plant wasn't about being the guy in charge, but an opportunity to make an eternal difference and to help others go Outside. That opportunity remains.

There are lots of questions that people have of me and maybe some that I even have of myself. I don't let it bother me. I just keep going each day with what God shows me to do. That's sort of what happened with this book, and now I'm an author too!

The first thing I did when I realized my personal journal was developing into a book was to build a team to help me figure out what was next. God brought all sorts of people together. We began to pray about the "book" being more than just a "book," but a real-life trigger for others and their story in Jesus. Our team is hoping and wondering:

What if thousands of "everyday" people, got up and headed Outside to change the world?

What if Going Outside was more than just a collection of ideas and theories, but real life stories?

What if a community of Outsiders could mentor and help other reluctant people go Outside?

What if more people came to know the love of Christ because Outsiders started playing their part in God's story?

So far, the reaction has been encouraging. People are sharing ideas and hopes for their relationships, careers, and communities with me. Some cry. Some laugh. They wonder aloud. Some look up and with frustration say, "It's time for me to do something!" They are tired of flinching. They are ready.

Their responses are the reason this book is sitting in your hands.

Writing *Go Outside* was a therapeutic and creative process. I tried to be intentional and take my time. This won't surprise you, but it's the first book I've written. Go easy on me.

The Outsider Movement is simple.

We believe that God is tapping the shoulder of everyday people like you and like me—creatives, entrepreneurs, and even hesitant starters. He is motioning to us, with a grin on his face, asking us to step out of our comfort zones and join him where the action is. He is inviting us Outside.

"For the bodies of those animals whose blood is brought into the holy places by the high priest as a sacrifice for sin are burned outside the camp. So Jesus also suffered outside the gate in order to sanctify the people through his own blood. Therefore let us go to him outside the camp and bear the reproach he endured. For here we have no lasting city, but we seek the city that is to come. Through him then let us continually offer up a sacrifice of praise to God, that is, the fruit of lips that acknow edge his name."

Hebrews 13:11-15

ACKNOWLEDGMENTS

For a project like this one, it takes a community of people to see it through. Rachel and I offer sincere gratitude to the following people for making *Go Outside* a reality:

To Jesus Christ, our Lord and Savior.

To *all* of our family. Especially my father and mother, Alton & Phyllis Webb. Thank you for a lifetime of consistency and support.

To Blake Lawyer, the pastor/elder team, and staff at Christ Community Church for taking the leadership and vision forward for our church family. Y'all rock. Seek the city.

To the people of Shelbyville, Kentucky. Thanks for believing in my family and rallying around the vision of going Outside.

To the entire team at the Fedd Agency. Thanks for believing in me and the Outside vision of Hebrews 13. Who would have thought horse shoes and a few FaceTime chats would have started such a deep friendship?

To Karl & Susan Babb for being our mentors. None of this would have existed if you didn't help us stay focused on Jesus and His equipping.

To Mark Watts. You taught us how to listen, love, and never judge.

To Jay Hardwick and family. In Jesus, proximity and time don't stop best friends. Thanks for the steady backing.

To Stacy Smith Rogers for helping me get my early thoughts together on paper. Such a great encourager!

To the Nashville Road Trip Team and to those who read early copies of the manuscript. You affirmed that this vision was special and that my dreams should be bigger.

To the many friends and mentors who have influenced and encouraged us over the years. You know who you are! We love you.

To all the Outsiders mentioned in this book. Thanks for allowing me to share your stories and their impact in my life. You continue to inspire me. Keep going.

ABOUT LEE WEBB

In 1997, Lee Webb was an entrepreneur with a dream to open his own business. As a CCIM designee, Lee has developed, sold, leased, or consulted on behalf of numerous local, regional, and national groups. He remains passionate about main street development and has assisted hundreds of owners and investors in purchasing their first building or taking that next big step. His company continues to serve the central Kentucky market with a passion to provide personalized and professional real estate services.

In 2009, God called Lee to be a church planter. He was the initiating and lead pastor for Christ Community Church (CCC) in Shelbyville, Kentucky. CCC didn't start from a traditional mold. Lee didn't go to seminary, and his wife, Rachel, never really imagined herself being a traditional pastor's wife. Driven by Hebrews 13:11-15, Lee and Rachel decided to explore the idea of joining Jesus Outside of their comfort and deeper into their hometown. Once they ventured "Outside" with a team of people committed to the same journey, they'd never be able to go back inside. Lee and Rachel were prayed over and sent by their former church to establish a church launch team in October of 2009. From the beginning, CCC focused on serving others and wondered together, "What does sincerely loving God and loving people look like?" CCC officially opened Sunday gatherings on 10-10-10.

From a small team gathered in a local paint store, CCC (loveshelbyville.com) and its leaders have grown to minister and share the good news about Jesus to several hundred people through the week and on Sundays. CCC is partnered with numerous outreach groups serving locally and internationally. These partners offer food for the hungry, shelter for the homeless, mentor and nurture children, assist in orphan care, and provide disaster relief—all to make a difference while sharing the love of God.

Lee continued his work in real estate while leading the church on a volunteer basis for five years. Leadership multiplied and he joyfully stepped aside as lead pastor. He is currently aspiring to be the world's best husband, father, mentor, and children's volunteer—and mediocre author.

Lee and his wife, Rachel, have three kids: Walker, Warren and Wells. Lee and Rachel became the first couple to individually win the University of Kentucky Alumni Association Young Alumni of the Year award (2010 and 2014). They are most known for their uncanny ability to find babysitters at the last minute, build epic forts in their family room, coach pee wee soccer, and function on very little sleep.

ENDNOTES

1. Hinton, S. E. *The Outsiders*. New York: Viking, 1967. Print.

2. Frost, Robert. Complete Poems of Robert Frost. New York: Henry Holt and Company, 1949. Print.

3. *The Maze Runner*. Dir. Wes Ball. Perf. Dylan O'Brien and Kaya Scodelario. Twentieth Century Fox Film Corporation, 2014. DVD.

4. Successories, Inc.

5. http://www.chucknorrisfacts.com/chuck-norris-top-50-facts

6. Burns, Ken. "James Roosevelt - The Roosevelts: An Intimate History." *PBS*.

7. http://www.pewinternet.org/fact-sheets/social-networking-fact-sheet/

8. http://insights.newscred.com/9-content-marketing-myths-busted/

9. http://gomin.org/about-go/history/

10. The Money Pit. Dir. Richard Benjamin. Perf. Tom Hanks and Shelley Long. Universal Pictures, 1986. DVD

11. http://www.entrepreneur.com/article/83560

12. Garrow, David J. *Bearing the Cross: Martin Luther King, Jr., and the Southern Christian Leadership Conference*. New York: W. Morrow, 1986. Print.

13. Russell, Bob, and Bryan Bucher. *Transition Plan*. Louisville, KY: Ministers Label, 2010. Print.

14. James Allan Francis. *One Solitary Life*, pp. 1–7 (1963).

NOTES

NOTES

NOTES

NOTES

NOTES

NOTES

NOTES

NOTES